Systematic evaluation

Systematic evaluation

METHODS AND SOURCES FOR
ASSESSING BOOKS

KENNETH WHITTAKER, MA, FLA

Principal Lecturer,
Department of Library and Information Studies,
Manchester Polytechnic

CLIVE BINGLEY   **b**   LONDON

Z
689
.W56
1982

Published by Clive Bingley Limited, 16 Pembridge Road, London W11 3HL, and printed and bound in England by Redwood Burn Limited, Trowbridge, Wiltshire.

First published 1982

British Library Cataloguing in Publication Data

Whittaker, Kenneth
    Systematic evaluation methods and sources for assessing
    books. — (Outlines of modern librarianship)
    1. Book selection — Methodology
    I. Title   II. Series
    025.2'3   Z689

    ISBN 0-85157-344-4

Typeset by Allset in 10 on 12 point Press Roman

1234568685848382

CONTENTS

LIST OF FIGURES

ACKNOWLEDGEMENTS

I should like to thank my colleagues in the Department of Library and Information Studies, Manchester Polytechnic, for their comments and suggestions and, particularly, Mr A G Pate, for reading and checking the work at the typescript stage. Above all, I should like to thank my wife for the help she gave me in the typing of the manuscript.

For permission to reproduce the pages from books and periodicals that make up the figures, my thanks go to the following people and organizations: the editor, *School librarian* (figure 1); the editor, *Growing point* (figure 2); the British Council (figure 3, *British book news*; figure 9, *Aids in the selection of books*); National Book League (figure 4); Edward Arnold (Publishers) Ltd (figure 5); H W Wilson Co (figure 6, *Current book review citations*; figure 7, *Book review digest*); and A J Walford (figure 8).

PREFACE

The ability to assess a book's suitability for addition to a library's stock, and in what quantity, is an essential quality for all librarians, and it is therefore a quality which has to be developed in all student librarians. I believe that there is a need for a book that will help students to recognize and develop this ability, in the same way that A M L Robinson's *Systematic bibliography* (London, Bingley, 1979) helps them to compile bibliographies. I have for many years taught students of librarianship about book evaluation, and this book is a development of my teaching experience. However, although this book seeks primarily to be a textbook for student librarians, its contents may have wider uses. Many of the chapters can be referred to by qualified librarians and used by them as a handbook to the evaluation aspects of book selection. In addition, its contents can be used by teachers and should also prove of value to anybody who has to write a book review, for evaluation is obviously at the heart of book reviewing, as well as book selection.

It is true, however, that book evaluation is only one part of the overall subject of book selection, and indeed only one of several stock evaluation processes with which librarians are concerned. Book selection has many aspects and the decision to buy a particular title is affected by such factors as subject specialization and library co-operation — for example, if a book is not available through a library co-operation scheme, is it worth buying it specially?

The subject of book evaluation is here dealt with in the following way. The first two chapters give the background information necessary for understanding and undertaking the evaluation methods which are suggested. The next three are concerned with systematically evaluating books. Chapter 6 deals with sources of information that the assessor may wish to refer to, for example, a reviewer's opinion on a particular publication. The last two chapters are short, the aim of each being to indicate further areas where the assessment methods advocated may prove of value. Chapter 7 discusses how the systematic approach to evaluation can be extended and used when books in a library's stock are being considered for withdrawal, that is, the book weeding process. The last chapter briefly raises the subject of non-book (and indeed non-print) materials, and how they, too, can be systematically evaluated (though it lacks the detailed discussion afforded to books in the earlier chapters).

I hope that this book, in addition to helping develop book assessment skills, will increase the interest of the library profession in general, and library school students in particular, in the selection and evaluation of books. Certainly, except with children's librarians, it is in this country a neglected area of professional activity. How neglected and therefore undervalued is suggested by the results of a survey of library school students by P Kohn reported in the *Assistant librarian* 70 (4) 64 in 1977. This revealed that only 1% of the students surveyed considered that book selection was a subject essential to their future careers. It is, of course, a subject, essential to the careers of the majority of professional librarians, and therefore a subject that should form part of the education of all student librarians. It is, further, a subject of particular importance in times like the present, when library book funds are being generally cut.

Kenneth Whittaker
July 1981

Chapter 1

CRITICAL APPROACHES TO BOOKS

The assessment scene

Books are assessed for more reasons, on more occasions, and by more kinds of people, than is often realized, and though in these pages assessment will be looked at from a librarian's point of view, it is useful to begin by setting the scene generally. If we examine the life cycle of a book we will find that it is assessed on a number of occasions during its life from various critical viewpoints. Of course, the pattern of evaluation will differ to some extent from book to book, but overall it will follow the course here indicated.

The first time a book is assessed is before it even becomes one. This is the evaluation carried out on the author's manuscript when it has just been received by the publisher. If the publisher decides the book is not worth publishing it is forthwith rejected, and so never sees the light of day unless it is subsequently offered to and accepted by another publisher.

When an accepted work is nearly ready for publication, it is evaluated for the first time as a book proper. At this pre-publication stage copies of the book (sometimes unbound) are prepared as inspection copies and sent to booksellers. Each bookseller examines his copy and assesses whether the title is one worth stocking. The accompanying promotional material sent by the publisher tries to persuade him, of course, that it is.

At publication, the book is evaluated a second time, for it is at this stage that review copies are sent out to book critics. Each critic peruses his copy and decides whether the book is worth reviewing, and if it is his review is published (or broadcast).

As the book appears on bookshop shelves and displays following publication it is evaluated again, this time by potential book buyers. These bookshop visitors may include librarians, though many have examination copies sent by library suppliers to their libraries and so do not need to visit bookshops.

11

Once the book has been purchased it is evaluated as it is being read. With books purchased by libraries, this evaluation will take place when the book is first borrowed, and then takes place again and again as the book is read by subsequent borrowers — probably over a period of years. A personal copy of a book, too, may also be read and evaluated several times, being lent to other members of the family and to friends.

The final evaluation of a book is made when it is decided to throw the book away. Of course, if the book is not actually thrown away, but sent to a jumble sale, or sold to a second-hand book dealer, then the final day of judgement for that copy is still well in the future. The copy will go through a further round of evaluations, as it is again sold, and again read, and may go through several such rounds as a second-hand book before finally being destroyed.

Evaluation plays an important part in the life of a book, because it occurs at so many stages in its life. It is also important because of the effect of that evaluation on the success and reputation of the book. Although it is probably true that the influence of book reviewers is less than they would like it to be, the cumulative influence of all the evaluations carried out on a book during its lifetime is enormous. Indeed, the book's life to a large extent hangs on the results of the assessments that it undergoes. And so authors, publishers, booksellers, and many other groups of people involved with books in one way or another, await the results of a book's evaluations with interest and sometimes with concern. Overall, evaluation can be said to be a necessary and essential part of book-world activity, and a process that is at the heart of the continuous interaction that must exist between the book industry and the book reading public.

It should be noted, however, that the assessments carried out on a book complement and even contradict each other. This is not just because people differ in their opinion of what makes a good book. Assessments can also be carried out from quite different points of view; for example, a scholar will think a second-hand book worth buying because of its contents, a book collector because of the way that it is bound. Both the contents matter and the physical appearance of the book are important, however, in most circumstances.

Selected approaches

The librarian's assessment of books is then but one of the many that take place and his approach is just one of a number. The features that are significant to the librarian when he examines a book differ markedly from those important to some other readers — including reviewers, whose reviews a librarian sometimes finds disappointing. This chapter now surveys a number of common approaches, all distinctly different, and indicates the selection and evaluation factors important to each. Even so, any user of books may adopt different critical approaches at different times.

The bookseller has a distinct approach to books because of his job — he sells books rather than reads them. This means that his main concern must be with which titles will sell and give him a reasonable profit. Thus he evaluates books more by their potential popularity than by their quality. He will select his stock from information sent to him about current publications and he will hope not only that what he chooses will not gather dust on his shelves, but also that he has not overlooked any titles that are going to be in demand, for customers will often prefer to go elsewhere for a title rather than wait for it to be ordered. Besides choosing titles, the bookseller also has to judge the quantities in which to buy them — too many and he will not be able to move them, too few and he will waste time in re-ordering.

The student reader often has his books selected for him, in his reading lists or advised by his teachers. This may mean that he is automatically more critical of the books he uses than if he had been able to choose them himself, though he will certainly be appreciative of any book he feels is clearly helping him with his studies. He will, however, expect his books to be designed in such a way as to make study easy, for example by including summaries and aids to memory. Nevertheless, his overall approach is not a particularly evaluative one, as he trusts his teacher to suggest the right books for him to read.

The general reader, adult or child, reads books mainly for pleasure, and reads them regularly. As well as buying books they are usually library members, as well as borrowing books from friends. The main factor in their evaluation of a book is a simple one; it is whether they personally liked it. They are not usually concerned about a book's finer points, but they will certainly form a definite overall opinion about each book they read. Their choice of book is usually by genre, for example a detective story, or because it is by an author they like (and whom they have probably read before). They may also read a book on personal recommendation by a friend. Sometimes they will choose a book for its illustrations rather than its words, and children in particular are, of course, avid users of picture books. Book reviews seldom play a large part in their choice of books — though the more

13

serious reader will probably take note – and they are likely to be more susceptible to the aggressive promotion of current titles in the media, and their prominent display in bookshops. Many general readers are good browsers, and find much of their reading material by chance whilst browsing in both bookshops and libraries.

The book collector, like the general reader, wants good value when he buys a book, but unlike the general reader his purchases will not normally be of new books. The books he buys he may read, but he buys in order to add to his collection rather than for reading purposes. Indeed, some collectors are not even book lovers, but collect old books as a way of investing their money.

Both personal and general factors are involved in making a book interesting and valuable to a collector. The two personal reasons are: is the book in his special field, and does he already have it? More generally, for a book to appeal to collectors it must satisfy the following criteria. First, is it an important book; that is, is it significant in its subject field, or written by a major author such as D H Lawrence or Jane Austen? Second, has the book rarity value? A book of which only a few copies were made, or still exist, is obviously more attractive, even though it may be expensive. Third, what condition is the book in? A unique item might be acceptable to a collector no matter the state it is in, but old books must normally be in first-rate condition in order to satisfy the collector's requirements. Books which have been damaged or neglected, and even books in good condition but which have been rebound, or otherwise changed from the state in which they were first published, are much less collector's pieces. Fourth, has the book any special features or interest? First editions of books are, for example, of particular interest to book collectors, whilst copies of titles signed by the author or having similar notable features are also of particular appeal to them.

The book collector of course will not find book reviews of much use to him when it comes to book selection. He must use his own knowledge, and through browsing in antiquarian (ie the better class second-hand) bookshops, through attending book auctions and through scanning auctioneers and second-hand booksellers' catalogues, make his decision as to what to buy for his collection.

Librarians are not normally called as part of their job to be book collectors of the type we have been looking at, but sometimes they are. For instance, the library in which they work may be building up a collection of rare and antiquarian books. University and research

14

libraries often build up such collections. Librarians, when book collectors, obviously approach books from the collector's point of view, and such a viewpoint can be seen in action in the fascinating writings of that collector librarian Lawrence Clark Powell.[1]

The bibliographer may be concetned with the tracing and listing of books, but more typically he examines books in a scholarly way, throwing light, as a result of his examination, on the history of books and printing, or on bibliographical aspects of a particular subject field, such as English literature. The need for such bibliographical work is succinctly brought out by Fredson Bowers, one of the most famous of all bibliographers, in his contribution to *Pages 1*.[2] In it he says, discussing English literature, 'just about every edition of the literary classics ... is corrupt, with departures from what the author actually wrote that may swell into the thousands in small details, but with enough major corruption in the words themselves to distort the sense and give cause for serious concern'.[3]

The bibliographer tries to establish a definitive or correct version of the text of a literary classic by comparing its various versions and printings. As well as looking at the actual text itself, he will examine as a physical object the book in which the text is printed. This kind of examining and comparing not only allows corrupt texts to be improved, it enables other more purely bibliographical problems to be solved, such as establishing the date of printing of a work. It has also been used to unmask literary and bibliographical forgeries. For example, a publication claiming to be a unique copy of a first edition of a work might be proved by a bibliographer to be a forgery because it is printed on a kind of paper that was not in use at the time the work purported to be published.

It can be seen than that bibliographical research is a type of detective work, painstaking in its approach and fascinating in its results. Although its results are probably of more interest to the book collector than the librarian, some librarians, like those with rare book collections, are certainly concerned with what bibliographers discover and may indeed do some bibliographical analysis themselves. But though only a few librarians are also analytical or critical bibliographers it should be remembered that most bibliographical research takes place in libraries. The main British journal in the field of bibliography, that of the Bibliographical Society, is therefore appropriately named *The library*.

The literary critic's approach and that of the bibliographer overlap as they are both concerned with the detailed examination of the text-

15

matter of books. The literary critic, however, is usually only concerned with works of literary merit, such as poetry, plays and novels, and his evaluation of them is essentially on literary grounds. He is looking to see, for example, how the writer uses such devices as metaphors and similes, how the book's plot is constructed and how alive are its characters. He studies particularly the great writers of the past, but he also is concerned with modern ones that he thinks are worth his attention.

The student of literature is expected to understand the literary critic's approach, and is, moreover, expected to use it in his essays. The literary critic himself will publish scholarly books and articles which incorporate the findings of his evaluation. These are very much more detailed than the critical comment found in a typical book review. Two famous twentieth century literary critics are F R Leavis who edited *Scrutiny*, a journal of literary criticism, and the poet T S Eliot, who wrote such critical studies as *The use of poetry and the use of criticism*. Introductions to the literary critic's approach are amongst the titles suggested in the guide for further reading at the end of the book.

Subject specialists include academics, research workers, and practitioners in such professions as medicine, architecture and engineering. They need to use books as part of their job, and so books (and other forms of printed materials) are important to them professionally. They will often write books as well as reading them, and they may also write (as well as read) book reviews for academic journals in their subject fields.

The subject specialist will select the books he reads partly from the reviews he sees in academic journals, but also from other information he sees about books, for example in publishers' catalogues. In addition, he will sometimes choose to read certain books in his field because they have been recommended (or written!) by his colleagues at work. As he will be concerned with keeping his subject knowledge up to date, many of the books he selects to read will be recently published works.

The subject specialist particularly evaluates the subject content of what he reads. That is, he is more concerned with the information the writer has put over, rather than how well he puts it over. He is also concerned with the authority of the author as this will affect a book's subject content. He expects the book to be written either by an established authority in the subject field, or by a writer who can clearly show through his use of his sources and through the research

16

techniques he employs that the information given in his book is to be trusted.

It should be remembered that librarians are subject specialists when it comes to books on librarianship, and that they adopt the subject specialist's approach when, for example, they are asked to review a new librarianship publication for one of their professional journals.

The book prize panelist's approach is one which some librarians also have to adopt as there are a number of prizes for books of distinction awarded by the Library Association, and they may be on one of the committees that choose the prize winners. Of course, most book prizes are awarded by publishers and literary foundations, though some are awarded by commercial firms. The book prize panelist's approach is different from virtually all others in three ways. First, the panelist will often have the books from which he has to pick the award winner already chosen for him. In the case of the Library Association awards, any Association member is entitled to nominate appropriate books, and so the panelists begin by having in front of them titles suggested by members, and it is from these titles that they would be expected to make their award. Second, it is a group approach, that is, it is one made by a number of people working together, and thus it results in a group, not a personal, decision being made. Third, it is an approach that has to be carried out within the rules and procedures laid down for the awarding of the prize. For example, the Library Association's most well-known award, the Carnegie medal (for the writer of what is considered to be the outstanding children's book of the year), has certain controlling conditions and these are laid down for all to see in the Library Association's yearbook. Sometimes the regulations that have to be followed include a list of the criteria by which the panelists have to assess the contending books. Such lists are, in fact, laid down by the Library Association in connection with their awards.

Journalists, as book evaluators, are those critics who write or broadcast book reviews for the media. The best known journalist reviewers write either for the 'quality' Sundays and Dailies or for a serious periodical of fairly general appeal, such as *The listener*, and the audience they write for is the educated general reader. Not all such reviewers are, in fact, full-time journalists, but they are normally full-time writers of some kind, perhaps writing poetry or biography when not penning their reviews. These journalist reviewers select what titles they will write about from the review copies sent by publishers to newspapers and magazines. Many of these critics choose to review identical titles,

17

as they like to write about those new books which look like being best-sellers. However, they may also review a book because it has a personal appeal to them, and certainly some of their reviews contain a strong autobiographical element.

Journalists, as you might expect, try to write interesting reviews, and usually succeed. Indeed their reviews can often just be read for pleasure. Their reviews, however, are not often systematic, and therefore seldom cover every aspect of the publications they review. But when evaluating a work, they will usually cover at least such points as the book's author, its scope, and its literary quality.

The journalist critics must affect the book selection habits of the general reader, but by how much it is impossible to say. Librarians, at least those working in public libraries, will certainly testify to the effect of this kind of book critic on some of their readers.

The social critic's approach to the selection and evaluation of books has developed in popularity in recent years, at least as regards children's books. It is an approach that judges a book on whether it is, in the eyes of the critic, likely to cause or perpetuate social musunderstanding and prejudice. The critic therefore particularly examines the writer's attitudes to matters like sex equality and race relations. The social critic's approach can be applied both to non-fiction books and fiction, but it has obvious limitations in that it hardly considers, for example, the literary merit of a publication.

An example of a children's author who has come under attack from social critics is the writer of the 'Dr Dolittle' books, Hugh Lofting.[4] These books are generally considered to be children's classics, but because of Lofting's attitude to coloured people, the social critics do not think these stories should be made available to readers any longer. It can be seen then the subject of censorship is relevant to any consideration of social critics.

Of course, social critics are concerned with books for adults as well as with those for children, and in the area of adult books the biggest argument is undoubtedly over pornographic publications. The discussion as to whether D H Lawrence's novel *Lady Chatterley's lover* is a literary classic or just pornographic rubbish seems to be over, but there are still people who are concerned about the way that sex is unnecessarily brought into some books, and feel that such books do indeed corrupt those who read them. Some social critics would probably therefore condemn all sexually explicit works.

Other social critics would probably condemn all novels below a

18

certain standard on social grounds. Some fiction, such as romantic novelettes, they argue, is not only badly written, it does its readers harm by acting on them like an addictive drug. These social critics therefore are amongst those who believe that public money should not be spent on buying such novels for public libraries. Similar critics of the novel have existed for many years, and indeed at the end of the nineteenth century they and public librarians discussed the subject at length. What became known as the great fiction controversy is still with us, and will probably never be resolved.

Librarians must take into account the reviews of the social critics. How much they should become themselves social critics is another question still to be resolved.

Teachers adopt a specific approach whenever they select and evaluate books for children in their schools. Of course, set textbooks are not normally selected by individual teachers, but most teachers do select books which they then may read to or use with their children. They come across such books in many ways, but they find that exhibitions and displays of books, such as those put on by publishers, are the best way of being introduced to what is available.[5]

Having found a publication which seems likely to be of use, a teacher will consider four points when he evaluates it more fully. Is the book suitable for children of the age he is teaching? Is the book suitable for children of the type he is teaching (for example, less able children)? Is the book one that the children will find interesting to refer to, to read, or to listen to? (For instance if it is a story book, could they identify themselves easily with the characters in the story?) Finally, is the book one of reasonable quality, perhaps indeed by an author of high reputation? Of course, teachers who are responsible for school libraries will approach books from a librarian's point of view as well as a teacher's.

The librarian's approach, like the teacher's, is determined by being concerned with the selection and evaluation of books for other people and not for himself. However, compared with the teacher, the average librarian has to consider publications suitable for a much wider range of readers. It should be noted, at this point, that a librarian seldom really selects all his stock. Sometimes he automatically buys material on a particular subject because he has agreed to under a joint library subject-specialization scheme. Sometimes he buys material because other people have the ultimate power over what is bought for the library. For instance, in public libraries the local authority committee controlling the library has the power to decide what is bought. Although it nowadays delegates this power to its professional library staff, as regards the purchase of individual books, it may still lay down a book selection policy (or framework) within which its staff must work.

Within any selection policy the librarian has to balance three forces, to some extent opposing, in his book selection practice. He wants to buy the best books, but he also want to buy those publications which are going to be used by his readers, and he wants, too, to buy the books which are the most economically priced. In trying to balance these forces he will take into account what he thinks of each book when he personally examines it, what reviewers of the book have written about it, and whether any of his readers have asked for the book to be bought. Incidentally, although librarians prefer to see the books they are considering buying, for example by having them sent by booksellers on approval, they often, for a number of reasons, buy some books they have only seen listed in a bibliography. There is a danger of course in this in that the book when it arrives may not be any use. But the librarian's experience means he can evaluate fairly accurately books that he has comparatively little information about.

When a librarian is able to evaluate a work by handling it personally, he will in his evaluation look at many points (they are all discussed later in this book). But compared with most other people who evaluate books, he will pay more attention to those factors that concern the way a book is arranged (including how it is indexed), and those that concern how it is printed and bound. This is because he wants books that he and his readers can get information out of efficiently (and well-arranged books make for this) and because he wants books that are suitable for library use (the loose-leaf form of publication for instance is comparatively unsuitable) and that will stand up to hard wear.

In conclusion two further comments are called for. First, when a librarian has decided he will select a particular book, he has not finished his job, for he then has to decide how many copies of the publication to buy. Second, when a librarian selects an item for his stock, he does not normally select it on the basis that he is going to keep it for ever. That means that, at a later date, he will be faced with the problem of evaluating it again, but in a different way. He will have to decide whether to discard it or not.

Notes and references

1 Especially recommended are Lawrence Clark Powell's *A passion for books* (London, Constable, 1959) and his *Books in my baggage* (London, Constable, 1960).

2 Bowers, F 'Recovering an author's intentions', IN *Pages: the world of books, writers and writing* (Detroit, Gale Research Co., 1976), pp218-27.

3 *Ibid.*, p218.

4 One publication that attacks Hugh Lofting that may be cited as being typical of the social critic's approach is *Racism and sexism in children's books* (London, Writers and Readers Publishing Cooperative, 1979), edited by Judith Stinton.

5 'How school teachers choose their children's books' *Bookseller*, November 7th, 1970, p2290.

Chapter 2

BOOKS: BASIC ANALYSIS

The language of books

Most of this chapter is concerned with covering fundamental information about books that all undertaking their evaluation need to know. As books are analysed first by type and then into their parts, many of the terms that are use in connection with books will be defined. However, there is still a need to begin with a general introduction to what may be called the language of books, that is, the specialized vocabulary used within the book world. All subject fields have such a vocabulary, and though the language of books is related to the vocabulary of librarianship, the two languages are distinct. The best work for quick-reference information on the language of books is Glaister's *Glossary of the book*,[1] whilst Harrod's *The librarians' glossary*[2] can also be recommended because it contains entries for book world terms. A third work of note, somewhat complementary to the other two, is John Carter's *ABC for book collectors*.[3]

The language of books is concerned with all branches of bibliography,[4] as well as other areas of knowledge such as printing and papermaking. It is a language which is widely used, and all readers (as well as writers) have at least a smattering of it. However, though it can be assumed that every reader knows what a page is, not all know that when a book is opened, the pair of pages revealed is known as an opening. Nor do they know that all right hand pages are recto pages and left hand pages verso ones. There is also a term to describe a pair of pages that back each other up; it is a leaf. So, for example, the title page of a book together with the back of that page form the title leaf. Similarly, most readers will know only a smattering of the abbreviations used as a shorthand for book world terms, eg ed. for edition.

Student librarians have a special need to know the language of books, not just in order to evaluate them, but because it is essential to other aspects of their studies, such as the study of

22

the history of books or the study of book design and production.

Besides including abbreviations and specialized terms, the language of books also includes those formalized descriptions of books that may be compared to the chemical formulae that form part of the language of chemistry. These formalized descriptions take several forms, and all are very relevant to library work. One is used in the making of bibliographical citations and references, a second in the making of catalogue entries, and a third, the most complicated, in the compiling of those detailed bibliographical descriptions of books that are undertaken for early printed works and some book collectors' items. A simple example of a collation (or physical make-up of the book) statement for a detailed bibliographical description follows. (An explanation of it will be found at the end of this chapter in the *Notes and references.*[5])

$$4° : \Pi^2 \ A - G^4 \ H^2$$

The example clearly reveals why such formulae are impossible to understand without appropriate knowledge.

It should also be remembered that foreign languages have their own specialized vocabularies and librarians concerned with foreign language publications therefore need to be familiar with the terms used in these languages. To help them a number of subject translating dictionaries are available such as the American Library Association's *The language of the foreign book trade*,[6] which covers fourteen languages. In addition to such dictionaries, they may find the handbook by C G Allen, *A manual of European languages for librarians*,[7] of use to them.

Types of books

Faced with evaluating a book the task is helped by knowing what category of book the work falls in, that is, what *type* of book it is. Defining and analysing the categories of book types is not a clear-cut process, however, and the first problem that arises is that of defining the term 'book' itself, since with some published materials it is difficult to decide whether at all they are books or not.

A dictionary will define the word 'book' along the following lines: a number of sheets of paper, fastened together and placed within a cover. This definition makes no mention of there being anything to read on the sheets of paper, because it is possible to have a book of blank pages, but of course it is usual to think of a book as being not just a physical

23

object, but one containing reading matter. It would seem reasonable to include as books, then, all booklets and pamphlets as, though they do not contain many pages, they are otherwise book like. On the same basis it would be reasonable to include books for the blind, for example in Braille, as these are read, albeit by the touch of the fingers and not by the eyes. On the other hand, talking books, taped recordings of the content of books, are not designed to be read, but to be listened to, nor are they physically like books. We should also exclude microcopies of books because their physical form is quite different from that of a book even though they are designed for reading. Finally, it would seem reasonable to exclude multimedia publications which incorporate materials such as film strips or cassette tapes together with a book.

But once we have decided what physically constitutes a book we are still faced with sorting out what goes in them. Books are made up of many ingredients. Their writers put into them variously imagination, information, wisdom and insight, ideas, intellectual and artistic skills, and emotions. The proportion of each ingredient will vary from one type of book to another, and from one title to another. But, as can be seen from the above list of ingredients, books have much to offer, and it is not surprising that they have been read and are still read by all sorts of people with all sorts of needs.

Non-fiction To the librarian non-fiction books are all those other than works of prose fiction, and include therefore works of imaginative literature like poetry and plays, as well as information books, even though such imaginative literature has much in common with prose fiction when it comes to evaluating it. In libraries, although non-fiction books are usually arranged differently and shelved separately from fiction, there are discrepancies between libraries as to what should be placed in each of the two categories. The average novel is automatically classed as fiction, but humorous books, if not strictly novels, may be placed either on the fiction or the non-fiction shelves, whilst novels in foreign languages (as opposed to translations) may be shelved in the non-fiction foreign literature classes.

Fiction This category of library stock comprises works of imagination in prose form, such as novels and short stories, including those historical or documentary novels based on real events or people sometimes referred to as faction. Titles like John Bunyan's *Pilgrims progress* may be also classed as fiction, though in some libraries these are shelved elsewhere with the non-fiction stock because of their subject interest, in this case religion.

24

Classics All great novels and other great literary works of the past are classics, but originally the term just referred to works by the famous writers of ancient Greece and Rome. Classic writings need not be literary, but exist for every subject field. For example, Charles Darwin's *The origin of species* is a classic of natural science. The classical works of all countries are frequently translated, and, because their qualities have stood the test of time, are frequently studied.

Textbooks Classics, though often set books to be studied in connection with literature examinations, should not be confused with textbooks. Textbooks are books designed to help students, normally working in groups under the guidance of a teacher, to learn efficiently. For this reason they include features such as exercises, examination questions and chapter summaries. Textbooks may be aimed at either children or adult students and be at any level from infant school to university. Public libraries seldom stock lower level textbooks, but try to provide a wide variety of those textbooks designed for students working on their own, rather than as part of a class. Many of these books for self-instruction teach their subject more informally than the typical textbook. Some textbooks, especially those on technical subjects, prefer to call themselves by another name than textbook, for example manual. Also designed for students — in fact they may be considered specialized forms of textbooks — are workbooks and readers. Workbooks complement textbooks by concentrating on the more practical aspects of appropriate subjects, for instance there are workbooks for students of cataloguing; readers (other than those used in the teaching of reading) complement them by bringing together in book form articles that students should read. The publications of the Open University are worth studying for the variety of textbook forms they show.

Standard works An advanced level textbook may also be a standard work on a subject, but standard works are usually more detailed and advanced than textbooks in their treatment of their topics, and contain more bibliographical references. Because of their authority and comprehensiveness, standard works, such as Bannister Fletcher's *A history of architecture*, will be found in all larger collections of reference books. The term standard author will also be found used, but in connection with imaginative literature. The works of such authors are of similar high quality to the information books entitled standard works.

Treatises This term may be used to mean the same as standard

25

work, but nowadays it has a more specialized meaning which relates to the field of science and technology. A treatise in these subjects is a very thorough treatment of a fairly broad area of knowledge. Perhaps the most famous in English is J W Mellor's multi-volumed *A comprehensive treatise on inorganic and theoretical chemistry*. Treatises, like standard works, are designed for the specialist rather than the student.

Monographs The word monograph is now sometimes used to mean any kind of scholarly work in book form (as opposed to articles in scholarly journals). However the term is more normally used to mean a book on a very specialized subject, written by a subject specialist, and designed for other specialists. Monographs, therefore, complement treatises and standard works, by giving fuller and more up-to-date treatment of narrower subject fields. They are very much research type publications, and many are issued as part of a publisher's monograph series, such as Methuen's *Monographs on physical subjects*. Any publisher's series is, of course, not only a number of books of a similar kind put out by a particular publisher, but ones published in a uniform style, and with an overall title like the above. A large series is sometimes termed a library as with the well known *Everyman library* published by Dent.

Books can be divided into types in a large number of different ways. To some degree, the way they are divided will depend on the critical approach being adopted towards them, and several such approaches were outlined in chapter 1. To a large extent library practice as regards dividing books into their types can be seen in the various sequences of books to be found in an average library. However, the stock of a library will also be found to be divided by size of book and by language, which is not examined here.

To the librarian, the most obvious basic division of books is, as we have seen, into fiction and non-fiction, and these two categories split naturally into two further ones, adult and junior works.

Breaking down each of these four categories in an appropriate way gives the following results. The junior or children's fiction group may be divided into story and picture books, and then the story books further divided into such classes as adventure stories, family stories, and animal stories. The adult fiction group may be divided into similar classes, for example detective fiction, historical fiction, and science fiction. However, there will also need to be some general fiction groupings like literary fiction or classical fiction. The traditional way

26

of dividing both the junior and adult non-fiction groups in libraries has been by a subject classification scheme, such as the Dewey Classification scheme. But increasingly, and especially for children's libraries, a rather less formal arrangement into subject interest gorupings has come to be used, as has always been a feature of bookshops. This kind of an arrangement places books under broad topics like countries, hobbies, and animals, and is most suitable for small collections of non-fiction books.

Subject classification schemes, although primarily dividing books by subject content, make allowance for the fact that some titles cannot be satisfactorily classified by subject but need to be arranged by their literary form. Poetry, drama and essays are obvious examples of literary forms, and clearly in the field of pure literature the form in which a work is presented is more important than its subject. But books on all subject may need to be classified by form once they have been classified by subject. For example, books of essays on art will be grouped together within the subject of art. It should be noted, in addition, that most types of quick-reference books are, like the essay, distinctive forms of presenting subject material. A listing of words on a subject, for example, is the dictionary form. Indeed quick-reference books as a whole are a distinctive way of presenting information, and so can be considered an overall literary form group within which there are a number of more specialized forms of presentation such as the dictionary form.

In libraries it will also be found that books are divided in one other basic way, into reference and lending stock. To the average reader, a reference book is a work such as an encyclopaedia or atlas. But these quick-reference books are, to the librarian, but one kind of reference work. Reference books to him are any books that cannot be borrowed from the library.

One further point on the subject of reference books should be noted. It is that librarians commonly divide quick-reference books in their reference stocks into two categories, bibliographical works, like national and subject bibliographies, and non-bibliographical ones, like dictionaries and directories. This is because the bibliographical work is more utilized by the library staff than by the average reader, being used in connection with, for instance, stock selection and ordering. For this reason, many bibliographical quick-reference works in libraries are separated from the non-bibliographical ones, and shelved out of sight in staff areas as opposed to on open shelves.

27

It is not always easy for a librarian to decide whether a book should be for reference or lending; it is even harder for him (or indeed anyone else) to decide on the nature of a book, and isolate its essential character, as experiments by the Public Library Research Group have shown.[8] Yet the categorization of books by their essential nature (a categorization mainly based on their aim and who they are aimed at) is important. Indeed, if such categorization were successfully achieved, it would certainly aid both librarians and all others concerned with the selection and evaluation of books. It would also help librarians in a number of additional ways. For example, it would help the compilers of book selection tools as they could indicate these categories as part of the information they give about books. It would also aid management investigations of library use, as the categories could be incorporated into reader surveys to help analyse the kinds of books being borrowed from libraries.

Probably the most fundamental distinction that can be drawn about the nature of a book is whether it is popular or serious.

Popular works, whether adult or junior, fiction or non-fiction, are easy to read, are read mainly for entertainment, and, if non-fiction, contain interesting rather than authoritative information. Popular works may be further divided by their nature into three groups.

i Sub-literature: This group of publications is poorly written, poorly produced, and usually only available in paperback. Because of its lack of quality it is seldom stocked by libraries, and indeed is more often sold by newsagents than by bookshops. Examples of sub-literature are romantic novelettes and many of the cheaper annuals put out at Christmas time.

ii Light literature: This group of publications is just worthy of being called literature. It is stocked by most libraries, and is avidly read by library users. The majority of historical, mystery, and similar stories come into this category, as do such non-fiction books as most people's tales of their wartime exploits and tales of sporting achievements.

iii Pictorial publications: This group is made up of children's picture books, which have pictures rather than text because they are aimed at young children, and of various adult pictorial publications. These adult publications, if well produced and of a large size, are sometimes called coffee-table books. Coffee-table, and those smaller books that mainly consist of illustrations, are eminently suited to be bought as gifts, but are less suited for purchase by libraries as they are designed to be looked at in much the same way as pictorial calendars.

28

Serious works set out to stimulate, inform, educate, or pass on experience rather than entertain, though they may do this too. They also can be divided by their nature into three main types.

i Academic information books: These publications are those information books designed either for subject specialists and research workers or for students undertaking courses of study. The main types of academic publications are textbooks, standard works and monographs (all of which have already been defined), and the academic group may be further divided by these types or by intellectual level.[9]

ii Non-academic information books: These publications are those information books designed for more general use, and aimed primarily at the general reader. There are two main categories of non-academic information books, those that deal with non-academic subjects like most hobbies, and those that take a non-academic approach to an academic subject in order to reach general readers.

iii Literary works: The third group of serious works does not include any information books, just works of the imagination. Those poems, plays, and novels which cannot be considered to be popular literature make up the majority of the contents of this group. It is therefore appropriately named literary works.

It is possible to divide up books in ways related to dividing them by their nature as A W McClellan has done with his functional approach,[10] and certainly if librarians are to select a balanced stock for their libraries, they need to understand precisely the role each category of book can play for their library users. They can undoubtedly learn something from the study that sociologists like Dr Mann[11] have carried out into the types of books and readers. Perhaps they can even learn something from that intriguing subject of biblio-psychology,[12] which tries to classify books according to their psychological characteristics, and readers according to their psychological types, in order to match one against the other, and so give the reader those books that meet his innermost need.

The parts of a book
Another approach to the analysis of books is separating out the various physical and printed features that they possess, and showing how each makes its contribution to the book of which it forms a part. Such knowledge of the parts of a book is needed in order to carry out a critical examination of a book of any kind.

Slip-case Few books have a slip-case, so it is a feature sometimes forgotten when the parts of a book are described. Books that have it are often referred to as boxed. The slip-case of a book consists of cardboard usually covered either with coloured paper or with plain cloth, and is just the right size for the book to slide into. After the book has been placed into its slip-case, its spine, with the book's author and title details, is still visible. That means that boxed books can be placed on library shelves as they are, if it is so wished.

The slip-case has two main functions. It protects the work (even though the book may have a dust-jacket as well) and it makes the book more of a showpiece. Books which are boxed are usually expensive works, like de luxe versions of the Bible, and so the slip-case helps impress the customer, and indeed gives him something extra for his money. Books which are in more than one volume, or which are part of a set, may also be boxed, and here the slip-case serves the additional purpose of keeping the volumes together as a unit. Incidentally, a multi-volume encyclopaedia may be sold complete with book-shelf for the same reason. Occasionally, the slip-case contains a special feature, such as the magnifying glass which comes with the miniprint version of the *Oxford English dictionary*. Occasionally too, it may be designed in a special way, as with Stone's *Justices' manual* where the slip-case takes the form of a carrier bag complete with handles.

Book jacket The paper-jacket or dust-jacket is a familiar feature of most bardback books. It should not be confused with the sealed cellophane wrapping which some books are now given, and which means they cannot be opened for browsing purposes. The jacket protects the book it is wrapped round, but nowadays its attractiveness is generally considered more important than its protective qualities. Libraries usually laminate book jackets or put a plastic jacket over them so they themselves are protected, and their attractiveness kept despite being repeatedly handled. Paperbacked books, though they are occasionally found boxed, do not have or need book-jackets, the information that jackets give being on their covers. The information about a book on its jacket will often be integrated into the jacket's overall pictorial appeal. Indeed the informative and pictorial aspects of the jacket can so overlap that it is the design rather than the words that communicate, for example, that the publication belongs to a particular publisher's series.

The information a book-jacket contains is seldom limited to details of author, title, publisher, and series. The front flap of the jacket generally gives the price and often a publisher's blurb, which describes the work in such a way as to make it sound as attractive as possible. This blurb may be supported by extracts from favourable reviews of the book. The back flap can contain a continuation of this type of information, but the back of the jacket is more likely to contain information about other books by the author or from the same publishing house. It is not customary for the reverse of the jacket to be used in any way.

Cover The cover of a book traditionally consists of board (rather like cardboard but stiffer) covered either with leather or cloth. However, there are many variations to this practice, quite apart from paperbacks. There are books where the board is covered with plastic, books where it is covered with laminated paper, and books, often called flexi-covered, where the leather or cloth (usually backed by paper) is all that there is, the board having been dispensed with. Most of these variations are jacketless. There are also exceptions to the cover being the same size as the book itself. For example, there are publications, especially Bibles, with yapp edges. These extensions to the normal cover may, if floppy, be joined with a zip fastener, making the book look like a kind of bag.

The purpose of the covers of jacketless works, from both an artistic and an informational viewpoint, may be considered to be generally the same as that of book-jackets. However, there are some specialist hardback publications that, although they lack jackets, have covers which are not eyecatching, and which merely contain (usually on their front and repeated on their spine) brief author, title, and publisher details. The covers of hardbacks, can, of course, be made into works of art by a binder, but those covered with cloth have to make do with the attractiveness of printed designs.

Though the covers of hardback books are not noticeable for the information they contain, one piece of information that should be found on the back cover of works published in recent years is the publication's International Standard Book Number (see page 34). This, as well as such information as the price, may be given in machine-readable form.

Student librarians should remember that many books in libraries are not in their original covers, having been specially bound or rebound for library purposes (see page 40). They should also note that a few books, such as *Whitaker's almanack*, are available in versions with stronger covers specially designed for library purposes.

End-papers The end-papers, also known as lining papers, are pieces of strong paper, possibly coloured or patterned, which, in hardbacked publications, help attach the book proper to its cover. There are two end-papers, one at the front, the other at the end of the book, and, except when a book is opened, they remain folded down their middle. Half of each end-paper is pasted to the cover board, and the other half left free to look like a leaf of the book. Endpapers are generally left blank, though sometimes illustrations or maps are printed right across them. Librarians prefer to have the end-papers blank, as illustrated ones pose problems if the book has to be rebound, quite apart from causing problems when the library labels the book.

Preliminary matter The items in a book which precede the text proper, and there can be many, are its preliminary matter or preliminaries ('prelims'). Together with the items that follow the main text-matter (the end-matter) they make up what is called the odd-matter or oddments of a book. However, these items are far from oddments in the sense that they contain considerable and important information. The items of preliminary matter differ to some extent from book to book, but they have a fairly constant order. In spite of their name and placing, they may be typeset or printed after the rest of the book, and can therefore be paginated separately, using roman numerals.

i *Blank leaves* In a hardback book, that half of the front end-paper which is not stuck down may appear to be its first blank leaf, but strictly speaking it is not part of the preliminaries. However, next to it, there may be one or more blank leaves, depending, usually, on the need to make up an even working of pages for the printer.

ii *Half-title* The first printed leaf contains on its front the half or bastard title. It should be noted that this feature, like the other important preliminaries, is given a right hand (ie recto) page, so it can be more easily seen. Though the half-title page usually contains only the book's title, and that often in abbreviated form, it may also contain the series title, whilst in novels the page may include a few lines outlining the plot. Quite apart from the information it gives, this leaf serves another purpose: it protects the title page.

iii *Announcement* The verso (ie back) of the half-title leaf may be left blank or carry a frontispiece, but often it announces other books by the author or other titles in the same publisher's series.

iv *Frontispiece* The frontispiece is a full page illustration that faces the title page. If it is not on the verso of the half-title page, it will be printed on the verso of a leaf or special paper, inserted because of its greater suitability to the printing of illustrations.

v *Title page* Although pride of place on this page is given to details of author and title, the name of the publisher almost invariably appears at the bottom of it, and the address of the publisher and the date of publication may also be found there. It is the title page details of a book which form the basis for library catalogue entries, and in cataloguing any variant forms of the title (for example on the book's cover) are ignored.

vi *Title page verso* The amount and variety of information now carried by this page is considerable as can be seen by looking at it in this book, and student librarians could well study a selection of such pages and note all the kinds of information they find on them. They should choose recently published works for this exercise, as the amount of information carried by the title page verso has increased over the last few years.

The information traditionally found on this page consisted of date of publication; statement of editions; name and address of publisher; and name and address of printer. (The name and address of the publisher and the printer must appear, by law, somewhere in the book.) This information, excluding the statement of editions, is known as the imprint.[13]

Of the other pieces of information now found on the title page verso, the following items are indicative: names and addresses of agents or co-publishers in other countries; information on the book's production, for example the kind of paper used; the copyright owner, date, and a statement about copyright infringement; the International Standard Book Number (ISBN); and cataloguing-in-publication (CIP) details.

A fuller explanation is called for of three of these pieces of information. They are the statement of editions; the International Standard Book Number; and the cataloguing-in-publication data.

The statement of editions is a list of past printings of the work. All editions — and a new edition normally indicates a revision of the work — will be listed. The statement may also indicate the printing dates of impressions, that is, the copies of an edition run off at a particular time, and the dates of the printing of reprints. (A reprinting is necessary when the original typesetting is no longer available.) The statement of editions may also indicate that the edition is of a special kind, for example, a limited edition; that is, one the number of copies of which has been deliberately kept to an artificially low number. Aimed mainly at book collectors, such editions usually have each individual copy numbered, that number also being given on the title page verso.

33

The International Standard Book Number (ISBN) is a ten digit number that identifies and acts as shorthand for a particular priced version of a particular title. The number is especially valuable now that computerized systems are being used in the book trade. It has four elements; one identifies the book's geographical, national or language group, the second its publisher, the third its title, and the last is a check digit. A space or hyphen is left between each of the four elements. In the example below the group digit '0' signifies one of the major English language countries (which include Britain and the USA).

0 241 89897 8

The cataloguing in advance of publication (CIP) data is information provided to help cataloguers, compiled usually from a proof copy of the work. In this country the cataloguing is done by the British Library and in the United States by the Library of Congress.

vii *Dedication* This is also occasionally found on the title page verso, but is more usually found on the next page. Dedications are normally short these days, eg 'To my wife'. There is a tendency towards replacing them with an appropriate quotation, though some books have both.

viii *Foreword* Although the terms foreword and preface are often used interchangeably, the word foreword is the one best suited to indicating introductory words about the book and its author written by another person, usually somebody of note. The words of the foreword, therefore, commend the book to the reader.

ix *Preface* This term is the one most suited to indicating introductory matter written by the author. Because of this the preface is of particular value to the evaluator. If a book has gone through several editions, a preface to each of these editions may appear. On the other hand many novels contain no prefaces at all. The preface is sometimes the last item of the preliminary matter. It may then be called the introduction, but that word is best used to serve another purpose.

x *Introduction* There is need for a distinctive term to describe introductory matter that appears in a book's preliminary pages that is not by the author or by a person of note, but is by the editor of a particular version or edition of an author's work. The word introduction should be chosen as this term. Introductions of this kind, which are particularly found accompanying literary classics, give background information on the author of the book and how it came to be written, together with comments on what literary critics

34

have written about the work and what the editor thinks of it.

  xi *Acknowledgements* The author's acknowledgements to those people and organizations that have helped him in writing his book often form a separate item of the preliminaries. Acknowledgements relating to the book's illustrations may be found incorporated with the publication's list of illustrations and not with the rest of the acknowledgements.

  xii *List of contributors* Those books that are by a number of contributors may have a separate preliminary item devoted to them.

  xiii *List of contents* Though novels often lack a list of contents, a contents page is an important aid to the reader (and so to the evaluator).

  xiv *List of illustrations* The illustrations, sometimes arranged by type, are usually listed in full. However, in some books no list at all appears of them, whilst in others the list of illustrations is select.

  xv *Corrections* Also known as corrigenda or errata, this information forms part of the preliminary matter because, as has been already mentioned, its items may be printed after the textmatter. In some books corrections are instead inserted into the book in loose-leaf slip or page form.

  xvi *List of abbreviations* In books where a list of abbreviations or symbols is called for, it will generally found towards the end of the preliminaries.

xvi *Guide to using* In many reference books and some other publications it is necessary to explain to the reader how to use the work. For example a dictionary may need to explain how the information in its entries is arranged and how it shows pronunciations. The guide may be entitled 'Key', and may also take diagrammatic form.

  Textmatter Because the textmatter of books is so varied, it is only possible to make a few general observations here.

  i *Visual information* The most obvious feature of the text pages of many books (other than the text itself) is the visual information of various kinds that supports the words of the text. In a few books, of course, the text supports the visual information, rather than the other way round. Visual information, when taking the form of illustrations, may be either line or half-tone. Line illustrations are ones like diagrams and drawings, where the illustration is made up of a series of lines. Half-tone illustrations, like photographs and paintings, are where every graduation of tone is simulated by breaking down the illustration into a series of minute dots. Half-tone illustrations may be printed on special paper separately from the rest of the book, and so given a separate

35

pagination. Illustrations produced in this way are commonly called plates. The brief descriptive information that accompanies any illustration is known as its caption.

ii *Pagination* The page numbers may be placed at the top or bottom of the page and they are normally given in arabic numerals.

iii *Headlines* Normally those at the head of left hand pages give the title of the book, those at the head of right hand ones the title of the chapter.

iv *Notes and references* Notes and references are particularly a feature of academic publications. The distinction between notes and references is that notes consist of supplementary information to that in the text, whilst references consist of details of other publications that the writer of the text has drawn on, for example for a quotation. However, though notes basically contain a different kind of information from references, the two kinds of information overlap, and so notes and references usually go together in books. They may be placed at the ends of chapters, the end of the whole book, but frequently they are to be found (normally in smaller type) on the text pages as footnotes.

Notes and references have to be keyed, of course, to the text, so that the reader can refer to them quickly from the text. Nowadays this is usually done by each note or reference having a running number. However, the traditional method is to use a series of symbols known as reference marks. Six of these exist, and they have to be used in a set order: asterisk (*), dagger (†), double dagger (‡), section mark (§), parallel (‖) and paragraph mark (¶). This method is still sometimes to be found, and is especially useful when notes and references are separated. For example if the notes are positioned on each page of the textmatter, whilst the references are given only at the end of chapters, reference marks may be used for the notes, leaving the running numbers for keying the references.

In second-hand books, in addition to the author's notes and references, manuscript notes by previous owners of the book may appear in the margins.

v *Thumb index* This is particularly valuable in quick-reference books, and its guide words or letters enable any required section of the textmatter to be speedily located.

vi *Bookmark* This may be in the form of a small linen ribbon, as with Bibles; on the other hand, it may take the form of a narrow piece of stiff paper incorporating advertisements, as with some directories and yearbooks.

End-matter The items at the end of a book are also commonly called the subsidiaries and may even be found entitled the back-matter. Some books, particularly works of fiction, lack most of them, whilst the order of them is much less rigid than that of the preliminary matter. However, there are many items that may be found in the end-matter. The order in which they are given here is the one in which they will usually be found. It should be noted that in a few publications all the illustrations are gathered together at the end of the book and may therefore be considered an item of the end-matter.

i *Appendices* These give in full documents, such Acts of Parliament, which would have interrupted the textmatter if placed in it; they give material supporting the textmatter such as tables of statistics; they give quick-reference information such as a table of weights and measures; they may also be used by the author to enable the full story of some event mentioned in the text to be told. It can be seen that a book may need a number of appendices, and indeed in a few publications a separate volume is called for to accommodate them.

ii *Glossary* This item is most common in books on technical subjects. For example, many books on computers have glossaries of appropriate terms.

iii *Notes and references* If these are placed in the end-matter, they will be normally divided by chapter.

iv *Bibliography* Bibliographies differ from lists of references in that the works in them are not keyed to particular places in the textmatter. Bibliographies can serve two completely different purposes. First, they can serve to reveal the sources that the author has used to write his book. Such bibliographies are therefore called lists of sources. Second, they can serve to guide the reader to further titles that he may read. Such bibliographies may be called booklists, reading lists, or guides to further reading. This second kind of bibliograpy is usually much more select that the bibliography of sources. The entries in these select bibliographies are, as a rule, more detailed though than those in bibliographies of sources. Both kinds of bibliography are likely to be divided by topic or by type of material, though they may be divided by the book's chapters. Indeed, in some publications there are reading lists at the end of each chapter rather than a single list at the end of the book. Bibliographies may be preceded by a few lines of introduction telling the reader the purpose of the bibliography and also how to use it.

v *Indexes* Indexes rather than index is the heading as many books have more than one, and half a dozen is exceeded sometimes. It should be noted that in some books the index gives more information than might be expected. For example, many atlases have what are called gazetteer-indexes, in which each index entry includes brief information on the geographical place itself. Some indexes, like bibliographies, will have brief introductions, guiding the reader into using them efficiently. Multi-volumed works can have, in addition to indexes in each individual volume, a general index at the end of the set.

vi *Supplement* This may contain material that the author would have placed in the textmatter had be known about it at the time of writing, or be a way of updating a book rather than by the production of a new edition.

vii *Colophon* In the early days of printing, the colophon was an important part of a book because books in those times lacked title pages, and it was the colophon that gave the information now found on the title page. Today the colophon, if there is one at all, will probably carry no more than the details of the printer with perhaps some information concerning the book's production.

viii *Advertisements* Books of Victorian and Edwardian times carried advertisements of all kinds which are now often more interesting than the books themselves. Advertising of other titles produced by the book's publisher is still found, but is less common than it used to be.

ix *Blank leaves* Just as blank leaves may be found at the front of the book, they may be found at its rear, and usually for the same reason. Sometimes otherwise blank pages in the end-matter are headed 'Notes', and offer an official place for the reader to put his manuscript additions to the publication.

x *End-paper attachments* The rear end-papers are commonly used to attach material to the book that will not fit (or be appropriate) elsewhere. They are the best place for fitting a large folded map, or a pocket of some kind. Pockets can hold a variety of material, and nowadays they are sometimes used for appendices in microfiche form.

Additional volumes and other separate parts The contents of a publication may be divided between a number of physically separate parts. The most obvious example of this is the publication published in a number of volumes (either together as a set, or one at a time). Such publications sometimes have in the end-matter to each volume a statement such as 'End of volume 1', so that there can be no doubt that the volume is only part of a larger work.

A less well-known type of publication, which also has a number of physically separate components, is the one that is published in sections.

38

Books published in this way may name their sections, as does the *Oxford Latin dictionary*, fascicules. The sections, which are of about pamphlet thickness, are usually issued irregularly.[14] Similar to this type of work are those pamphlet-like publications, usually of a popular and encyclopaedic nature, issued at frequent and regular intervals. In fact, although these publications build up into considerable works, with a number of loose-leaf binder volumes, each binder housing a few of the sections, they are often considered periodicals rather than books. Certainly their sections are usually sold by newsagents rather than bookshops, but these works when complete are basically like a multi-volumed book.

Very different from books published in many sections or volumes, are those works that have just one separate part. An obvious example of this is the book that has some pages of corrections issued loose with it rather than bound into it. There are also a few publications that have other material issued loose with them. For example Spirt's *Library/media guide* has a 'Teacher's key' that takes this form.

Finally it should be remembered that the multi-media works mentioned at the beginning of this chapter may have a number of physically separate components, but such works fall outside this chapter's definition of a book.

A book must go through several stages before its component parts are ready to be put together. After the publisher has accepted the author's typescript, it will be edited, and the illustrations, if not already with it, added. The work will then be typeset (these days usually by computer-aided typesetting) and proofed to check for any errors. Proofs may be unpaginated (when they are known as galleys) or paginated (page proofs). It is only when the page numbers are known that the index can be compiled. The preliminary matter can also now be completed with the page numbers being added to the lists of contents and illustrations.

This description is based on a typical hardback publication, which normally has paper jacket, cover, end-papers, and book proper, or body of the book. The paper jacket is obviously wrapped round the book after it has been assembled, but it is less obvious to see how the other three components are assembled. However, because library books are well used, they sometimes begin to come to pieces, and it is then possible to see how they have been made. Their disintegration normally starts with the front hinge of the book giving way. (The hinge is where the front end-paper folds to let the book open and close.) Once this has happened, it is easy to see how the book has been made, for the cover of the book is partly detached from the book's body as soon as the hinge has broken. If the rear of the pages (they are only now revealed) are examined, it will be noticed that they are folded into groups, known as sections. It will also be seen that the sections are attached to each other by twine. Pull at this twine, and the sections will come apart. The main reasons for the pages (or leaves) being gathered into sections are first that it makes for strength, and second, the presses that print the book do it several pages at a time on large sheets of paper that are then folded down to page size. The final size and shape of a book is its format. The names folio, quarto, and octavo, which most people associate with the size of books, are really to do with how many times the original printed sheet of paper has been folded. A sheet folded just once to give two leaves (or four pages) produces a folio book, a sheet folded again to give four leaves (or eight pages) produces a quarto book, a sheet folded a third time to give eight leaves (or 16 pages) produces an octavo book. Nowadays many books have sections of even more pages, eg 32, 64, 128.

After the sheets have been folded, the resulting sections have to be placed in order so that the binding of the book can begin. To help the binder know the order of the sections, each is usually given a distinguishing mark known as a signature. These traditionally take the form of the letters A, B, C, etc, and these letters are placed in the margin at the bottom of the opening page of each section. Therefore in an octavo book, a signature mark should appear on pages one, seventeen, thirty-three, and so on.

When the sections have been placed in their correct order they are stiched together, and the end-papers of the book attached to the first and last sections of it. If the illustrations in a book are printed on different paper from the textmatter, the leaves or sections of illustrations have to be inserted before the main sections of the work can be stiched together.

The body of the book is now made ready to receive the cover. Covers, when made separately from the body and only attached to the body at virtually the end of the assembly process, are known as cases. Before the cover is attached, the body of the book is usually trimmed (if it is not, a paper-knife has to be used to open the folds and allow the pages to be read), and has its spine shaped, glued and strengthened. The cover is attached to the body by the pasting of that part of the end-papers that comes in contact with the cover. It is further attached by there being underneath a portion of the end-papers a piece of muslin-like cloth known as mull. This is glued both to them and to the book's spine. With cased books, the cover will already have had any lettering or decoration that is necessary printed on it before it is attached to the body of the book.

There can be variations on this process. When books are assembled by hand, for instance, it is usual for each book's cover to be individually made, and for it to be attached to the body not just by glue but by tapes which are worked into the cover boards. Books made in this way cannot break at the hinge as cased works do.

Another fault that may be found in books today is that individual pages fall out. This is because they have been bound by what is now usually called adhesive binding, but what was at one time inappropriately named perfect binding. With this form of binding the pages are not in sections but just attached as single leaves to the spine.

Although most books are bound in one of the above ways, some will be found assembled more unconventionally. For example, their pages may just be stapled together, or they may be placed in a loose-leaf binder, or they may be kept together by some form of spiral binding (circles of wire or plastic). No doubt, as printing becomes more computerized and more books are produced by non-traditional processes, the physical parts they will possess, together with the ways they will be assembled, may become even more varied.

To conclude, it should be remembered that whilst all book evaluators need to know something about how books are assembled and bound, librarians are also concerned with their rebinding, for libraries have to send many of the items in their stock away for such treatment.

Notes and references

1 Glaister, G A *Glaister's glossary of the book: terms used in papermaking, printing, bookbinding and publishing, with notes on illuminated manuscripts and private presses* 2nd ed. London, Allen and Unwin, 1979.

2 Harrod, L M *The librarians' glossary of terms used in librarianship, documentation and the book crafts; and reference book* 4th ed. London, Deutsch, 1977.

3 Carter, J *ABC for book collectors* 6th ed. St Albans, Granada, 1981.

4 Five branches of bibliography may be distinguished, though they overlap to some extent. They are physical bibliography (or the

making of books), historical bibliography (or how books used to be made), systematic bibliography (or the listing of books so that there is a record of their existence), analytical and descriptive bibliography (or the careful examination and detailed recording of books), and critical or textual bibliography (or the scholarly use of the results of analytical and descriptive bibliography).

5 $4°$ = quarto sections.

Π^2 = Unsigned opening leaves (half sheet of two unsigned leaves).

$A-G^4$ = Seven sections of four leaves (or eight pages) with signature letters A to G.

H^2 = Half sheet of two leaves with signature letter H.

Note: Total number of leaves in the book 32 (ie 64 pages).

6 Orne, J *The language of the foreign book trade: abbreviations, terms, phrases* 3rd ed. Chicago, American Library Association, 1976.

7 Allen, C G *A manual of European languages for librarians* New York, Bowker, 1975;

8 Jones, A and Pratt, G 'The categorisation of adult non-fiction' *Journal of librarianship 6*(2), April 1974, pp91-8.

9 A discussion of the nature of books with particular reference to the subject of their intellectual level will be found in a publication of the International Federation of Library Associations (IFLA) entitled *International target audience code (ITAC): a proposal and report on its development and testing*, by Russell Sweeney, 1977.

10 McClellan, A W *The logistics of a public library bookstock* London, Association of Assistant Librarians, 1978. See also his 'Decision problems in book selection' *Library review 29*, Winter 1980, pp235-46.

11 Mann, P H *Books, buyers and borrowers* London, Deutsch, 1971. See also his work with J L Burgoyne, *Books and reading* (London, Deutsch, 1969).

12 Simsova, S *Nicholas Rubakin and bibliopsychology* London, Bingley, 1968.

13 Librarians, however, do not normally include the printer's name and address in the imprint part of catalogue entries.

14 If a section or other small part of an already published book is subsequently published on its own it is known as a separate.

Chapter 3

THE SYSTEMATIC METHOD

The systematic method of evaluation introduced in this chapter can be used to assess books of all kinds, and to evaluate old books (including second-hand ones) as well as new. True, it is not really designed for books which are more of value for their collectability than their contents, but the basic method can be used with them too. It can also be applied to materials other than books, such as periodicals. Though specially designed with library school students in mind, it is relevant to any librarians who have to carry out the assessment of stock. Indeed, it is hoped the method will prove of use to all who have to undertake book evaluation, and not just to library and information workers.

There are twelve stages that together make up the full systematic method, though it is possible for certain stages to be omitted, depending on the objectives of the evaluation and the time available for it.

Here, we shall introduce them all, although some of the individual stages will be dealt with in detail in later chapters.

1 Objectives	7 Comparable publications
2 Strategy	8 Personal conclusions
3 Background reading	9 Obtaining second opinions
4 Criteria	10 Obtaining further information
5 Examination	11 Final results
6 Matching	12 Applying results

Objectives
First, the objectives of the evaluation must be defined. Every evaluation is carried out for a particular reason, for example a student has to present a project, or a librarian has been sent a book to review by the editor of a journal. The objectives of the assessment must be borne in mind throughout the whole of the evaluation process, since they obviously affect the nature of the assessment. If ever the exact purpose of an evaluation does not seem clear, and it is difficult to know what to

do, the evaluation should be halted until the objectives have become clarified.

The usual reasons for undertaking an evaluation, at least in the library world, are either professional or academic. Professional librarians obviously undertake evaluation mainly for reasons connected with their job, and do it not only when carrying out book selection, but at various other times as when assessing whether a publication will answer a reader's enquiry. They seldom, however, have sufficient time to be able to carry out as detailed an assessment as they would like. Students of librarianship undertake evaluation for academic reasons, though their assessment should be geared to library situations and professional needs. They are more likely than professional librarians to be able to devote as much time as is needed to carry out a detailed evaluation.

Strategy

Having decided on the objectives, it is then necessary to work out a strategy for the evaluation that will allow those objectives to be met. The basic strategy described here can be adjusted to meet individual circumstances, depending, for example, on the time available for the assessment, or the experience of the evaluator.

Background reading

Strategy having been established, it may be necessary before the evaluation process goes any further for background reading to be undertaken. However, this stage need only be undertaken if the evaluator feels that he is lacking some knowledge essential to the evaluation. Thus, if he has to assess a book that is to do with a subject on which his knowledge is limited, he can turn to works like encyclopaedias in order to improve his knowledge, and therefore his evaluation. Then again, he may want to know more about the criteria useful in book evaluation, and may consult publications such as this one. Finally, if he is a student librarian, for instance, he may want to find out more about the kind of work he is evaluating, for example, if it is a dictionary, more about that particular kind of quick-reference book. He can then turn to textbooks or handbooks on types of printed materials such as the Library Association's publication, *Printed reference material.*[1] Instead of resorting to printed sources the evaluator can, of course, also remedy his lack of knowledge by consulting knowledgeable people directly.

Criteria

Next, the evaluator must decide what criteria, that is, standards against which the publication can be judged, should be applied to the evaluation. The criteria that he eventually selects, such as up-to-dateness, accuracy, and depth of indexing, will vary, depending on the kind of book under assessment. For example, those appropriate for evaluating novels will obviously differ from those appropriate for quick-reference books. The choice of criteria will also be affected by the purpose for which the assessment is being undertaken. Though lists of suitable criteria may be created by the evaluator to suit his particular needs, it is often easier to use existing lists such as those found in various books and articles aimed at librarians.[2]

Criteria to suit most purposes, and relevant to most types of publications, are listed below. These headings, which have been given a logical order, should be easy to remember. They are the framework around which it is suggested evaluators should build up the criteria they choose for each evaluation they undertake.

1 People Many people, in addition to the author, are usually involved in the creation and making of the work, such as editors, illustrators, and designers, and the evaluator must take their performance into consideration.

2 Plan Every book has a framework or foundation upon which its contents have been built — whom the book has been written for, and what subjects it covers — which must be examined.

3 Contents The main textmatter of the book must be considered in respect of such points as, for example, the author's style and the work's use of illustrations.

4 Organization This deals with the arrangement and indexing of the book, which are, of course, more important in information books than in novels.

5 Design The book's contents, organized as the author desires, should be laid out both efficiently and attractively when the book is published.

6 Production This deals with such features of the publication as the quality of the materials of which it is made, and the standard of the actual printing.

7 Placing This involves the overall impression given by the book, and summarizing its standing in comparison with other publications.

The criteria needed to assess books of different kinds are treated in detail in later chapters, as this stage of the systematic method, together with the examination stage, form the heart of the evaluation process.

Examination

In addition to what is written here and in later chapters on the examination of books, it should be remembered that much of the information in the last chapter is also relevant to the examination stage. The standards against which the assessment is being carried out, must, of course, be borne in mind throughout this stage, and if, during an examination, it is realized that the criteria need adjusting, it should be done immediately.

Book examination can be carried out very thoroughly, and in these pages this approach is entitled 'The Full Examination'. Such an approach would obviously be the one likely to be chosen by a book reviewer writing for a scholarly journal. However, briefer examinations are often more appropriate and more practical, as in most library book selection situations. Two varieties of shorter examinations may be distinguished. The longer one of the two has been given the name 'The Skilful Skim', and the shorter one called 'The Experienced Glance'.

During all examinations, mental notes must be made of what is found, and in all but the briefest examinations it is recommended that written notes be made of all important points.

– *The full examination* This type of examination is the kind that not only reveals most about the work under evaluation, but teaches the student librarian most about book selection. It is normally the kind of examination required when the evaluator has to put his findings in writing, although it should be possible to write a few lines about a work without giving it the full examination treatment. Comprehensive examinations are seldom carried out when books are being selected for individual libraries because of the time they take, hours rather than minutes. A full examination will be most efficiently carried out if the following procedure is adopted.

i Preview This will take no more than a few minutes. The object of it is to enable the evaluator to obtain an overview of the publication, and decide on the criteria that will be important to bear in mind during the examination. The preview may also serve another purpose: it may enable the evaluator to decide whether it is worth continuing any further with the examination. For instance, a book reviewer working for a newspaper will usually have a number of books sent to him to write about from which he has to select a few to feature in his column.

46

Previewing all those that he is sent enables him to decide which he will feature, and will need to examine further. The others the preview allows him to reject.

Previewing consists of reading the information about the book on its dust-jacket and cover, examining its title page and the information found on the back of the title page, looking at the contents page, and at any other of the preliminaries that seem to have important matter on them, and then finally quickly thumbing through the textmatter and subsidiaries, probably stopping, however, from time to time, to glance more closely at anything that attracts the attention. This routine is virtually identical to the one used when carrying out 'The Experienced Glance'.

ii View The steps taken in order to carry out this main stage of the examination are common to all evaluations, though, of course, the precise procedure within each step is not. They are:

1 Deciding on arrangement of notes: A decision must be made as to the headings that the evaluator is going to use when he makes his notes. He may want to use headings that relate to parts of the book, eg dust jacket, but it is suggested that the seven terms put forward under which criteria may be grouped are the best headings to use here. They are, it will be remembered, People, Plan, Contents, Organization, Design, Production, and Placing.

2 Noting bibliographical details of book: The minimum bibliographical details that should be noted about the book under examination are author, title, edition (if other than first), and date of publication. However, it is useful if various other details are also noted, such as publisher and place of publication, together with price. If fairly full bibliographical details are decided upon, also note down the book's International Standard Book Number (ISBN), how many pages it contains, and, if it belongs to a publisher's series, the title of that series. In addition, if the book under examination is in more than one volume, its number of volumes must be recorded. Finally, if the book is in the stock of a library (as is likely with student evaluators), the library in which it has been seen, together with its class number, should be noted. Either the evaluator himself, or some reader of his evaluation, such as tutor, may want to locate the work at a later date.

3 Reading the book: The work should be read in the normal manner, that is cover-to-cover. (Of course, a quick-reference book cannot be read in this way and can only be sampled.) During the reading make any necessary notes, and, at the same time, record any page

47

numbers of the work that it may be necessary to refer to again. The approach of the evaluator to what he reads should be careful, critical, and considerate. It should be careful because, if it is not, important points will be missed. It should be critical because he is not just reading but evaluating the publication. Incidentally, it should be remembered that critical reading means appreciating the good qualities of a book, as well as seeing its weaknesses. Finally, the evaluator's approach should be a considerate one, in that he should read in a way that brings his heart into play and not just his head. Such an approach is obviously particularly relevant when imaginative literature, like a novel, is being read.

4 Carrying out tests and analyses: The last step within the detailed examination procedure is the carrying out of further investigations into the contents and features of the work. For example, a children's book might be tested using a Readability Index,[3] to ascertain whether its reading level suits the age group it is aimed at. With an information book, the testing might very well include a search for the latest dates to be found in its pages, and this testing might also cover the latest publication dates to be found in its bibliography (if it has one). As for analyses that can be carried out, these might relate to comparative treatment of subjects, if an encyclopaedia, or to the use of diagrams, if a technical book. The technique of scanning is particularly of value when carrying out tests and otherwise analysing books. Scanning is running the eyes quickly over the lines of print in the book until required information is located. It is the quick-reference kind of reading.

iii Review It may not always be necessary to review the book after the main viewing of it has taken place, but often it needs to be done, because otherwise something is forgotten and so omitted from the examination. Reviewing consists of looking at one's notes, and checking that there are no gaps in them. If there are gaps, the book must be looked at again, and the gaps filled in. Occasionally, reviewing may mean the rereading of part of the book, but usually it will mean no more than referring to the book a few times, and so can be done in a matter of minutes.

— *The skilful skim* Shorter examinations of a book, such as this kind, are easier to carry out when the evaluator has already experienced what it is like to carry out a detailed examination. The skilful skim is based on the technique of reading known as skimming, that is, reading selectively but covering and extracting all that is important. This kind

48

of examination should take less than an hour to complete, and indeed with experience can be carried out much quicker. It is the type of examination chosen by a librarian who is compiling a library booklist, in which each book is briefly introduced. The skilful skim consists of reading the book's dust-jacket, and cover, then looking fairly carefully at its preliminaries, and finally paying attention selectively to its textmatter and subsidiaries. A skilful skim will include reading any prefaces or introductions, looking closely at the start and the end of the main textmatter, and sampling the text elsewhere. It will also include spot-checking the book's index (if it has one). Lastly, it will include noting the work's bibliographical features (if any), and ascertaining the sources used by the author in the book's compilation.

– *The experienced glance* The experienced glance, as has already been stated, can be considered to be similar to the preview part of the full examination. It lacks depth, but it is often sufficient to enable an experienced librarian to gauge if he needs to buy a particular book for his library. This brief examination consists of looking at the book's dust-jacket and cover, at its title page and the information on the rear of the title page, at its contents page, and then glancing rapidly at the rest of the book's contents. If something in the book catches the evaluator's eye, he may browse at these pages, but such browsing is not really called for.

The examination stage, in order to be complete satisfactorily, needs to be carried out by a person with certain attributes. These are bibliographical knowledge, subject knowledge, well-developed reading ability, and empathy. Librarians have always had the first, as their working life is spent with books, and increasingly have the second as more and more of them are graduates. But the other two attributes they may not have, and though the librarian may be taught advanced reading skills such as the technique of critical reading,[4] it is not so easy to be taught empathy. Empathy may be defined as the ability to assume the identity of another in one's imagination. Foskett in his *Creed of a librarian*[5] suggests that in reference service librarians need to put themselves in the reader's shoes to do their job effectively. It is not only in reader service that librarians need this ability: in book evaluation empathy is just as necessary. The evaluator must be able to put himself in the author's shoes and in that way appreciate better what the author is trying to do, and why he has chosen the means he has to achieve his ends.

Matching

When the examination is complete, its findings can be matched against the criteria being used. In fact, the process of matching really takes place during the examination process, but it is only after the examination has been finished that the matching can be finalized for then the perspective is available to ensure accurate matching. Matching can be done mentally, but if notes are being made, they will form the basis for it. If the notes have been placed under the headings suggested, that is the seven terms under which the criteria are also grouped, then the arrangement of the notes automatically allows the matching process to take place.

Comparable publications

Making comparisons (and contrasts) between the publication under evaluation and other publications is an essential part of any thorough evaluation, though this stage of the systematic method may be omitted from shorter assessments. Comparisons may be made with other editions of the book under evaluation, as well as with similar works. It is essential that this stage is included in any thorough assessment as it is only when a book is looked at in relation to other existing publications that its strengths and weaknesses can be fully seen. However, this comparison stage is also valuable because it often reveals points about the book under evaluation that had been overlooked. If possible, more than one comparable work should be examined, but it is not usually worth while examining more than about three other titles. The examination of comparable publications will not, of course, be done in the same detail as that of the book being evaluated: it will probably take the form of a Skilful Skim.

Personal conclusions

It should now be possible for the evaluator to make up his mind about the book. The relevant evidence has been examined; all that remains is for some conclusions to be drawn from it. It must be admitted that sometimes they are more easily drawn than others, and so the evaluator may find himself unsure about them. If this happens, he should look again at the comments about the book that have been noted down, and after further thought try once more to reach some conclusions. If still unhappy, he should recall to mind the objectives of the evauation, as this may help. If he is still not satisfied, there is but one thing to be done, obtain the opinions of other people, preferably people with appropriate knowledge and experience.

Obtaining second opinions

This stage in the systematic method may be omitted from briefer evaluations, but comparing the evaluator's views with those of other people is an essential feature of comprehensive assessments. This stage should be left until after the evaluator has made his own conclusions, otherwise he may be unduly influenced by the other opinions he has obtained. Of course, in some evaluation situations, as in the case of books seen by librarians at book selection meetings, the opinions of others are automatically a part of the evaluation process, no matter how brief it is. There are two kinds of second opinions that can be obtained, the first the views of people such as other librarians, the second the opinion of reviewers as found in published book reviews.

1 People's comments: Ask a colleague or a friend for his opinion of the book. Preferably the person asked should be knowledgeable, though it may not always be possible to find a subject specialist. Student librarians should obviously try and obtain the opinions of professional librarians, and then compare them with their own. In particular, ask the people whose opinions are sought for their views on points about the book on which it has been found difficult to make a firm decision. If the person consulted does not know the publication asked about, he may be prepared to examine it, at least briefly, and then give an opinion of it.

2 Reviewer's assessments: Book reviews and other published assessments, if they can be traced, are especially valuable for second opinions. There are many newspapers, journals, and reference books that include assessments of all kinds of books. These sources form the subject of chapter 6.

Obtaining further information

It may be necessary, with a comprehensive evaluation, to trace further information about some aspects of the book, even when other people's opinions are to hand. For example, more facts about an author's qualifications may be desired than are to be found either in the publication itself or from other people. Fortunately librarians are trained to know where to find the answers to most questions, and so should be able to carry out an appropriate search and obtain the required information. For information about an author's qualifications, for

51

example, the obvious information sources are biographical dictionaries like *Who's who*, and failing them, indexes to biographical sources such as *Biography index*. It may even be necessary on occasions to contact the publishers of the book under evaluation.

Final results
The stage has now been reached when all the opinions and information collected concerning the publication can be put together. In particular, the evaluator's personal conclusions will be integrated with the results of the second opinions obtained, and the further information unearthed. Altogether, it should be found that there is available more than sufficient material and observations for satisfactory conclusions. However, there are frequently certain points about a book on which it is impossible to ascertain all that is sought. Do not be concerned about this, just accept that it may happen. With the final results then to hand, all that is left to do is to apply those results to the purpose for which they were obtained.

Applying results
This is the last stage of the systematic method of evaluation. There are many ways in which the results of a book evaluation can be used. Some of these applications are particularly relevant to student librarians, others more relevant to professional librarians, yet others relevant to workers outside the library world as well as to those in it. The applications will now be looked at in turn.

The rest of this chapter attempts a number of things. As well as showing how the results of a book evaluation can be applied, it tries to indicate some of the techniques needed to apply them and to suggest which of the applications are suitable for student librarians to perform. The applications are arranged so that those that generally need the most detailed investigation of books come first. Some pages from published evaluative sources are reproeced to illustrate points made.

Book reviewing
A book review is a published evaluation of a work which is designed to tell people about a book (usually a new one), and about the good points and the bad points that it possesses. It is therefore both informative and critical. A lengthy review may be difficult to distinguish
52

in content from a piece of literary criticism, but essentially a review is more concerned with introducing and recommending (or otherwise) a book to the reading public than with studying its literary characterstics such as the author's use of metaphor.

Librarians may carry out book reviewing for a number of reasons. They may be asked to review books for a publication put out by their own library, such as the Hertfordshire Library Service *Material matters*; they may be asked to review books on librarianship for librarianship journals; they may be invited, if subject specialists, to review books for subject journals. They may also be invited, incidentally, to take part in book discussions at professional meetings, or appear on radio and television book programmes (particularly on local radio), and on such occasions their reviews, of course, will be spoken not written.

Excluding such spoken or oral reviews, reviews of books may be grouped into five categories. They are mini-reviews, full reviews, review articles, omnibus reviews and survey-reviews. The librarian may have to carry out all the above types of reviews, but it is probably the mini-review that he is called upon most frequently to undertake. Reviewing sources aimed at librarians, like *British book news* and the American *Library journal*, consist in the main of such reviews, and so librarians needing guidance on how to write mini-reviews should study the reviews in these and other similar periodicals (see figure 1). The mini-review will typically be just one or two paragraphs in length. It will usually contain between one hundred and two hundred and fifty words. If in two paragraphs, it will probably have its opening paragraph describing the work, its second commenting critically on it.

Although mini-reviews are common in journals written by and for librarians, in reviewing sources aimed at most other kinds of readers, both general and specialist, the average book review is usually rather longer, about two hundred and fifty to one thousand words. This kind of review may be termed the full review. Reviews of this type allow the writer to include an extended description of the book, together with a more detailed assessment of it. This length of review may even include suggestions to the author of the book as to how the work may be improved if a future edition is ever published. It is a kind of review that can include brief quotations from the work under review, and it should certainly include some comparison of the book with other similar publications. An example of a periodical with most of its reviews of this type is the *Times literary supplement*. Library world examples are *Library review, Journal of librarianship* and many other professional journals. The reviews in the *Journal of librarianship* also include a few of article length.

The review article, sometimes called the review essay, is longer than one thousand words and such reviews are usually only found in learned journals, and then not frequently. Their writers are subject specialists, writing for other specialists within their subject field, and so can assume a knowledge of the book's subject field by their readers. A review article normally does more than just review the latest edition of a book in detail. For instance, it may investigate developments in the subject field of the book as well as writing about the book itself.

Both the omnibus review and the survey-review differ from the types of reviews already discussed in that they evaluate more than one book at a time. The omnibus review, frequently found in the review columns of newspapers, is where the reviewer takes two, three, even four recent publications on broadly the same subject and assesses them all at the same time (see figure 2). This has the advantage of allowing the reviewer to appraise comparatively, as well as allowing him to write about more titles in the space that he has been allocated.

The survey-review (or review survey) is one in which the reviewer takes not a few but a large number of titles on a certain subject, or related in some way, and briefly assesses each (see figure 3). Survey reviews are of article length, and the titles are dealt with in narrative form, as opposed to being listed with comments. The value of the survey-review lies in it allowing the reviewer to appraise all the books within the scope of his review in a systematic manner, comparing and grouping as he wants as he goes along. Survey-reviews are a feature of the already mentioned *British book news*, and librarians who are asked to undertake assessments of this type should study the survey-reviews in this publication.

No matter what type of review is being written, the reviewer needs to cover at least the following points. He needs to give the book's vital statistics, that is, its bibliographical details, including those of any variant versions also issued (hardback and paperback for example). He needs to indicate what type of book he is dealing with, if this is not obvious from the vital statistics. He needs to give any background information he thinks relevant, for instance, details of previous editions. Usually he needs to comment on the author, and certainly the author's aim must be stated. He needs to reveal the subject or theme of the work, together with whom the publication has been written for. He needs to mention the work's strengths and weaknesses, and should try to touch on as many relevant criteria as possible, though he may concentrate on a few. He needs to state where he would place the book in comparison with other similar publications. With reviews aimed at librarians, the reviewer should end by clearly recommending what kind of library ought to buy the work.

Reviewers should be seen to be fair to the authors of works they review, and they should also not make a review an excuse for airing their own favourite hobby-horses. They should angle their reviews obviously so that they meet the needs of their readers. As for the style of writing which they adopt, it should be simple rather than flowery, that is, they should write professional English rather than literary English. They must keep to the number of words given them, and to any other instructions that they have been asked to follow by whoever has offered them their task. Incidentally, though editors of journals frequently issue rules for contributors of articles, they seldom have any additional guidelines for their book reviewers.

Student librarians, when asked to write reviews, will normally be given by their tutors adequate guidelines. However, if they are given within these guidelines some choice in what they can do, there are many project ideas that they may consider, especially if they are undertaking a review article or essay. They can choose, for instance, to evaluate the works of a particular author, perhaps with especial reference to that writer's latest book. Or they can take a small number of comparable publications (not more than four it is suggested), for example, recently published titles on a topic they are interested in, and carry out a detailed comparative evaluation of them. They can also carry out a comparison on some works of a more specialized nature, such as encyclopaedias. They can examine how a subject (or subjects) is treated in several similar publications. For example, a foreign country might be selected for such a study. They can even take a particular title and trace the reviews that have been published about it, and then review the reviews.

Book selection
Book selection applications are here considered to be only those that relate to evaluating books for puchase by particular library systems. Like reviewing applications they too are many, but they may be divided into just three groups: first, the evaluation of books for book selection panels and meetings; second, the evaluation of books at book selection meetings; third, the evaluation of books in such places as bookshops,

library suppliers' showrooms and book exhibitions, or of sample copies on display within the library system.

The evaluation of books for book selection panels and meetings is a form of appraisal that allows librarians to carry out the thorough kind of examination that reveiwers undertake. Indeed, carrying out assessments for a library's own book selection meeting may reasonably be thought of as in-house reviewing. The report on the assessment may be given verbally to the meeting, or it may be given by filling in an assessment form. It is not usual for a book review like those found in reviewing journals to be produced, indeed in-house reviewing of all kinds is not common. It is probably carried out more by libraries in the United States than in Britain, where its use would seem to be almost restricted to children's books. A variation of the in-house review system is for the review written by the member of the staff to be placed with the library display copy of the book, which copy is then examined by other members of staff. An interesting American venture that features this practice is the Review and Evaluation Center of the Anne Arundel County Board of Education in Maryland. Here copies of books and other library and educational materials are displayed together with evaluations of them. These evaluations, incidentally, include not only in-house ones, but ones extracted from published review sources.[6]

Evaluation at book selection meetings will complement in-house reviewing in some library systems, in that the staff at the meeting will base their decisions on the in-house reviews they read or hear. However, at most book selection meetings, the appraisal of the books passed round will be carried out on the spot, and the decisions made without reference to reviews of any kind. On the other hand, at some book selection meetings, published book reviews may accompany the books under examination, whilst before many book selection meetings, the staff at them will have had a chance to look at the books, the titles having previously been on display. The books handled at book selection meetings may be ones of which the library has already bought a single copy, and so the meeting's decisions will relate to how many more copies the library system needs and where, or they may be on-approval copies sent by booksellers and library suppliers, who will therefore take back any titles that the library decides it does not require. A final point concerning the assessment of books at book selection meetings is that although it is not normally a detailed assessment, it is on the other hand a joint assessment. The meeting's decisions are made by a group of staff who together constitute a pool of knowledge

56

and experience that no single evaluator could match.

The assessment of books in such places as bookshops and of display copies in libraries is particularly important to librarians who are not able or entitled to attend book selection meetings. It is also important to those librarians who are in small or specialized libraries where it is not feasible to have book selection meetings, and where it may not be possible to obtain books on approval. The examination of publications on shelves and displays has the advantage over the typical book selection meeting in that the librarian can take as long as he likes over his appraisal. He will obviously have to make notes of the bibliographical details of the books he sees (unless a list of the works on display is available), and he may make further notes on them. Sometimes with the books on display there will be publishers' catalogues giving helpful descriptive information, and if a list of the works on display is available, it too may give infomation about the publications.

It should be noted that quite frequently librarians select books without seeing them, and so, of course, their evaluation of them is virtually non-existent (unless, that is, they use published evaluations as a substitute for evaluating a book personally). However, many libraries select books either just from seeing publishers' information (which admittedly is descriptive) or only from seeing bibliographical details of the work in a bibliography like the *British national bibliography*. Although experienced librarians can tell a lot about a book merely by reading its bibliographical details, such brief information, even though it may reasonably be termed (as earlier in this chapter) the book's vital statistics, can be misleading, and is certainly an inadequate base for efficient selecttion.

Student librarians should always practise book selection with the books to hand, and although the projects and exercises they can carry out normally have to be divorced from an actual library setting, there is still much that they can learn. An example of a book selection activity that they may undertake is a mock book selection meeting, preferably with problem titles, and within a given library setting. Such a meeting enables students both to evaluate titles, and to compare their views with other students.

Compiling book-guides

Book-guides is an overall term that may be given to those bibliographies and booklists put out both by commercial and institutional publishers and by libraries that give guidance on what to stock or read. Usually

Literature: Fiction

GUNN, JAMES (Editor) *The road to science fiction 3.* New English Library (Mentor), 1979, pp. 656, £1.75. Paper cover. 451 01784 6

This is a desirable purchase for librarians who cater for fifth- and sixth-form SF addicts and who find 656-page paperbacks viable. James Gunn has brought together thirty-six stories which illustrate the developing trend of SF from the 1940s to the present day, introducing the volume with a twenty-one-page survey, and prefacing each story with a two- or three-page account of the career and style of the author. My copy was stiff to open, but very sturdy.   NORMAN CULPAN

HUTCHINSON, DAVID *Torn air.* Abelard, 1980, pp. 160, £4.25. 200 72691 9

Although in these eleven stories figure instant matter transmission, universal telepathy, a visitor from space and, here and there, electrostatic fields of stupendous voltage awakening strange forces, they belong rather to the genre of the sinister macabre than to SF. Sometimes the characters verge on the sleazy and brash, a not uncommon affectation of youth; sometimes the language has considerable evocative power; and just occasionally the two tones jostle one another. Only nineteen at the time of writing these stories, David Hutchinson shows considerable promise. They will be enjoyed by most sixth-formers and some younger readers.   NORMAN CULPAN

Literature: Poetry

PRITCHARD, WILLIAM H. *Lives of the modern poets.* Faber, 1980, pp. 316, £8.50. 571 11618 3

To so entitle a book as to invite comparison with an earlier and greater work may seem presumptuous even for a professor of English, and an American one at that. The author, in his introduction, justifies his admitted act of pretension by affirming that juxtaposing the two helped him to put his own aim more clearly: to provide introductions to, and revaluations of, the nine most interesting and important poets (Hardy, Yeats, Frost, Pound, Eliot, Stevens, Robinson, Crane and Williams − a nice balance of English and American) writing in English in the first part of this century.

To reconsider poets, many already overburdened by commentary, may seem merely to add another stone to a rising cairn of criticism reflecting views and attitudes of their day; but established views must expect to face challenge, and many face it here. The author agrees with Eliot that Victorian criticism had become less purely literary and had merged with philosophy, aesthetics and ethics, while in modern criticism there was the very notable influence of psychology and sociology. The presumption that there are poems by great poets that have something to do with their own lives, and that poetry must be judged by what it is and nothing else, dictates the author's approach to biographical details and interpretations, and has resulted in a stimulating book of interest to student, specialist and general reader alike.   RAYMOND WARD

Figure 1   Mini-reviews in the *School librarian*

A WUTHERING OF WITCHES

JILL MURPHY *The Worst Witch strikes again* Allison and Busby £3.25. Ill. by the author 72 pages 8¼ x 7¼ January '80 0 85031 251 5.

JANET SMITH *The Wakeley Witch* Kaye and Ward £3.95. Ill. Peter Rush 124 pages 8½ x 5¾ May '80 0 7182 1237 1.

BRIAN BALL *The Witch in our Attic* B.B.C. £4.25. Ill. Jill Murphy 86 pages 8 x 5 December '79 0 563 17727 6.

MARGARET STUARY BARRY *The Witch of Monopoly Manor* Collins £3.95. Ill. Linda Birch 80 pages 9 x 6¼ March '80 0 00 184930 10.

JOAN CASS *The Witches' Lost Spell Book* Hodder and Stoughton £2.95. Ill. Ferelith Eccles Williams 91 pages 7⅛ x 4¾ June '80 0 340 24934 X.

JOHN BELLAIRS *The Letter, the Witch and the Ring* Hutchinson £4.50. Ill. Richard Egrelski 188 pages 8 x 5¼ February '80 0 09 139040 0.

Junior stories that centre on a witch are likely to be either comic, with the young reader encouraged to take a light view of the improbable aspect of magic, or sinister, with magic threatening to get out of hand. The kind of metaphor which Helen Cresswell achieved through Lizzie Dripping's sardonic apparition is rare in books for the young — rare, most of all, because of the complete integration of adult and child vision. In *The Worst Witch strikes again* (and its predecessor, *The Worst Witch)* the species witch is, as it were, humanised, and serves the same role as the animated scarecrow Worzel Gummidge in providing an outlet for the anarchic feelings of the young. Mildred, *enfant terrible* of Miss Cackle's Academy for Witches, is put in charge of a new girl in the hope that responsibility will steady her. Unfortunately blonde Enid's demure appearance is deceptive; her behaviour is as subversive as Mildred's but more capably disguised. It is a long time before anyone realises that the monkey who disrupts school discipline is her permitted cat-familiar under enchantment, and the spell which hurls Mildred through a window into a decorous tea-party at the end of her pole-vault is never brought home to Enid. However, Mildred does learn some sense by Enid's mischief, and the young reader learns something about cause and effect in a series of episodes in which teachers (soft, tough or sarcastic) and fellow pupils (loyal, quarrelsome or gullible) approximate with comic effect to the everyday life of any classroom. The racy humour of the book is supported by vigorous drawings that lend personality to the characters in terms of gentle caricature.

The friendship of a witch can be inconvenient. When Micky Potts and his sister Samantha find a shabby old woman living in a large cupboard on Pelham's Piece they are at first excited at the thought of getting to know a witch. But this one is in difficulties. She has lost the energy-beamer without which broomstick and spells alike have become inefficient and uncontrollable. While the children and their friends energetically search for this necessary magic machine, the witch enters enthusiastically into their lives. Broomstick rides at the village fête are a great success (the adults are content to offer ingenious scientific explanations for erratic flights which the local children take happily for granted), but her

3744

Figure 2   An omnibus review from *Growing point*

The British Novel 1976-1980

Martin Seymour-Smith

It would not be possible, in the space available, to mention all the novels that were published in this five-year period except by simply listing them, and thus saying nothing useful about them. I have reluctantly excluded short stories, detective stories, speculative (or science) fiction, and adventure fiction. I have chosen what seemed to me to be the most promising and interesting of the novels by new writers, and the more important of those by authors long established.

It is extraordinary that fiction continues to be published in the quantity it is. Libraries now buy fewer novels, and many of those individuals who used to buy fiction in hardback have been forced to give up the valuable habit, as publishers have been forced—much against their will—to raise their prices. But it is gratifying to be able to say that very few manuscripts of merit by writers who are as yet unpublished will fail to find a publisher—indeed, many books which do not deserve publication at all can, in

good-natured satire of modern ways (right, left and non-political).

At last Edward Upward's remarkable semi-autobiographical trilogy about the life of a communist so dedicated to his Marxist-Leninist creed that he breaks with the British party was published in one volume: *The Spiral Ascent*, consisting of *In the Thirties*, *The Rotten Elements*, *No Home but the Struggle*. In the early 1930s Upward, admired friend of Isherwood, was one of Great Britain's most powerful and successful surrealist authors, but, true to his creed, he broke with experimentalism and finally—after years outside literature—took up formalism (as he saw it). His trilogy is almost malodorously humourless and doctrinaire, and it is not always well written; but it has not yet been valued highly enough. It is a most dogged and truthful record of drab and repulsively unimaginative devotion to a loathsome cause: one made by a man of imagination, as Upward's early prose shows. It is one of

nervously and think; it is unlikely that this novel will eventually be seen as any kind of falling off. Like *The Pyramid*, it is naturalistic rather than overtly symbolic. Interestingly, it seems to suggest that homosexual love is purer than heterosexual love, a theme not obviously apparent in its predecessors. Like anything by Golding, possibly the most gifted of all living English novelists, this book will take some time to get used to.

Emyr Humphrey's *The Anchor Tree* is one of the finest of this somewhat neglected Welshman's many novels: with its twists and turns in time, and its involved but not recondite theme, it could teach many younger and more famous novelists a thing or two about technique. It manages to deal successfully and convincingly with three interwoven themes: the nature of eighteenth-century Welsh pietism, modern America, and Nazi war-guilt. By contrast P. H. Newby, in *Kith*, returned to the Egypt of the Second World War, and wrote his

Figure 3 A survey review from *British book news*

PEOPLE AND PLACES

47. Allen, Eleanor, **VICTORIAN CHILDREN**
A. & C. Black 1973. £1.95. 64 pp. illus. SBN 7136 1324 6
An intriguing book describing how children lived a hundred years ago, the
text and illustrations providing the details children love. There is a list of
interesting places to visit, and of books for further study.

48. Allan, Tony. **THE TIME TRAVELLER BOOK OF PHAROAHS AND
PYRAMIDS**
Usborne 1977. £2.25. 32 pp. illus by Toni Goffe. SBN 86020 08 3
This cheeky comic strip approach to history quickly engages the interest of
younger readers—the pages are colourful, varied and eye catching, and the text
provides just enough accurate information to hold the attention and show
what it may have been like to live in a remote time and place.

49. Boase, Wendy. **A CLOSER LOOK AT ANCIENT EGYPT**
Hamish Hamilton 1978. £1.75. 32 pp. illus. SBN 241 899052
It is worth looking at books in this new and enterprising series, and this one is
especially good, dealing with a subject which seems to fascinate generations of
young children. The dramatic aspects, such as the Pyramids and the cult of the
dead, are dealt with, and, in addition, there are interesting sections explaining
how so much is known about the Egyptians, and who were the archaeologists
who have discovered these sources. Very young children will enjoy just looking at the pictures. Older fluent readers will appreciate the text.

50. Brett, Bernard. **EXPLORERS AND EXPLORING**
Longman Young Books 1973. £2.50. 143 pp. illus. SBN 582 15060 4
Explorers and exploring are perpetually fascinating to young children. The
very young will enjoy looking at the black and white photographs, the
dramatic coloured drawings, while older ones will be absorbed by the well
chosen extracts from letters, diaries and journals of famous and lesser known
explorers.

51. Cockett, Mary. **ROADS AND TRAVELLING**
Basil Blackwell 1964. £0.85. 62 pp. illus by T. H. Strubley. SBN 631 06580 6
Though published ten years ago, this remains an informative little book,
tracing the development of roads from Roman to contemporary times. The
text is accurate, the pastel coloured drawings pleasing, the black and white
ones dramatic. Ordnance Survey maps are introduced, and something of their
fascination conveyed.

Figure 4   An annotated book-guide, National Book League's *Read
and find out: information books, 6-9*

these bibliographical compilations will have brief comments accompanying their entries, but sometimes, as with lists of best books, the mere fact that the work is listed in the publication is guidance in itself. Book-guides are normally concerned with books that have been published over a period of time rather than recent publications. They are used by librarians particularly when revising their stock or when selecting stock for new service points, and by readers needing advice on what books to choose for a particular purpose. Examples of book-guides put out by libraries are Sheffield City Libraries' *Basic reference books for the home* and, covering similar titles but from an American viewpoint, the Enoch Pratt Free Library's *Reference books: a brief guide*. Examples of book-guides put out by bodies other than libraries are the National Book League's *Read and find out: information books, 6-9* (see figure 4) one of the many book-guides available dealing with children's books, and the H W Wilson *Fiction catalog*. This United States compilation has a particularly interesting feature, the critical part of its annotations being made up of quotations from published book reviews.

The information and comments about a book that accompany entries in book-guides are known as critical annotations. (If there is no evaluative content in an annotation, just information about the book, then it is called a descriptive annotation.) Student librarians need to learn the art of annotation, which they may then use in undertaking bibliographical compilations such as annotated book-lists and bibliographies. The critical annotation consists of a few concisely written sentences on a book. Annotations aimed at librarians will emphasize why a book is worth stocking; those aimed at the reading public will emphasize why a work is worth reading. The critical annotation will normally include facts as well as comments, though if the book-guide it is in gives full catalogue entries there will obviously be no need to mention factual points such as the presence of illustrations. The annotation's information and comments should normally mention a book's author, its aim, its subject scope and its audience, as well as indicating the overall quality and usefulness of the publication. With annotations designed for readers, the spirit of the book preferably should be caught, especially if it is a novel. Annotation, in fact, is an art as well as a skill and the good annotation, because of its brevity, is perhaps even harder to write than the good review.

Assisting readers

Library staff carrying out assistance to readers use the evaluations in book-guides but they also personally evaluate publications for their readers. They do this in two main ways. They do it when they are asked to recommend a good book or a course of reading, and they also do it when they are asked for information and have to choose the best book that will supply it.

Recommending good books is often referred to as readers' advisory work. The evaluation that takes place here is unusual in that it is not normally based on an examination of titles following the request for assistance, but is based on the already accumulated knowledge that the member of staff possesses as a result of his library experience, and of the reading he has done of both books and book reviews.

Obtaining information from books is often referred to as reference work. This also involves evaluation of a rather unique kind. What is called for is not an evaluation of the book overall, but only an evaluation of it from the point of view as to whether it will satisfactorily answer a particular enquirer's question. In both reference work and readers' advisory work the evaluation that is carried out is a mental one, and so does not take much time.

Staff assisting readers may also carry out library instruction, that is, they teach readers, either formally or informally, how to use books and libraries. These staff, as part of their job, will therefore teach the evaluation process, instructing readers how to evaluate books, as well as evaluating books themselves.

Student librarians will be given the opportunity to carry out book assessment for reader assistance purposes by being given exercises in enquiry work including, perhaps, case studies. But it will only be when they are working in a library that they can fully develop their use of these applications of the evaluation process.

Book weeding

Book weeding is the examination of a library's existing stock to decide which titles should be kept and which withdrawn. Obviously, weeding books is related to book selection, being a complementary process. The criteria for book weeding differ somewhat, however, from those for book selection, as factors such as how much a work has been used since its purchase and its present physical condition are additional important criteria. Book weeding is discussed in a later chapter. The weeding process needs experience in order to be carried out effectively,

63

and for that reason, perhaps, it is not an activity in which student librarians are often asked to undertake evaluation.

Notes and references

1 Higgens, G, ed. *Printed reference material* London, Library Association, 1980.

2 An example in article form is: American Library Association, Reference Services Division, Bibliography Committee 'Criteria for evaluating a bibliography' *RQ 11*, Summer 1972, pp359-60. An example of a book with such lists is: Cabecieras, J *The multimedia library* New York, Academic Press, 1978.

3 J Gilliland's *Readbility* (University of London Press, 1972) is a work that could well be consulted, but chapter 5 (pp90-1) gives some information on this subject.

4 A fairly recent work on the subject is: Buzan, T *Speed reading* New edition. Newton Abbot, David and Charles, 1977.

5 Foskett, D J *The creed of a librarian* Manchester, Library Association, Reference, Special and Information Section, North West Group, 1962, p10.

6 Division of Library Developments and Services, Maryland 'State focus: recent developments in materials selection' *Library keynotes* 7(6), October 1977, p3.

Chapter 4

GENERAL CRITERIA

Rather than deal in turn with the evaluation of different kinds of books, which would be rather repetitive, the seven criteria group headings introduced in the last chapter are divided into those which are applicable to all kinds of books, and those which are not (depending, that is, as to whether it is information books or books of imaginative literature that are under assessment). In fact, only one of the group headings consists of criteria that vary depending on what type of book is under assessment, the heading that relates to content matter. In this chapter, therefore, the other six headings, People, Plan, Organization, Design, Production, and Placing, are all dealt with, since they comprise generally applicable criteria, whilst the heading Contents, though introduced here, is considered more fully in the next chapter.

It will be found that the criteria covered both in this and in the next chapter are considerable in number, because as many as possible have been isolated. Though some come close to overlapping others, all are worthy of individual attention. The criteria are arranged as logically as possible within the headings of which they form a part, and these are, of course, themselves in a systematic order.

The information given about each criterion endeavours to do three things: first, to explain exactly what the criterion is concerned with, together with its relative importance; second, to suggest how and where to test for it when a work is under examination; third, to indicate how the criterion relates to particular kinds of books. It will be found that the basic analysis of books made in chapter 2 is drawn on as we discuss criteria, and indeed some points made there will be mentioned again, but from a different angle.

It should be remembered that, although these criteria can be applied to all kinds of books, they will not all apply, of course, to every individual title. When assessing a particular title, the evaluator must therefore obviously decide what kind of a book he is evaluating before he can choose the criteria relevant to his examination.

People

This criteria heading comes first because it is people who think up the idea for a book, and it is people who carry through that idea until the work reaches publication stage. It is not always realized how many people are needed to prepare the average book for publication. In the case of multi-volumed works the size of the team of people needed can run into hundreds, sometimes thousands. The sort of people that make up the team will be revealed as the criteria in this group are individually explained. Obviously the people who write and produce a book will affect the quality and authority of that book. Unfortunately, it is not really easy for the evaluator to learn a lot about the people involved in a book's preparation, as even those mentioned by name in the work are, with the possible exception of the author, usually only identified by a bare name, or name and address. This means that, in order to assess the standing of the people who have written and produced a book, it is necessary to be sufficiently knowledgeable to recognize significant names whenever they are come across. It is true that it is sometimes possible to turn to biographical and other reference books to find out more about an author or book designer, but there is no real substitute for personal knowledge. It is recommended therefore that student librarians read the book-trade press and related publishers' literature, and also look at literary journals, as well as reading books on as many subjects and by as many authors as possible. It is further recommended that they not only talk to each other about books, but attend meetings and conferences at which they can meet and listen to people from other areas of the book world.

Author The author is the most important person concerned with a book, yet it is not always possible to know who is the author of a particular publication. This is not just because some authors prefer to remain anonymous, or alternatively, write under a pseudonym; it is because some books are works of corporate authorship. That is, they are published, for example, by a government department, and the author is considered to be that government department. In such works the name of the civil servant or other actual writer will seldom appear, in the same way as the name of a journalist often does not appear under a newspaper story.

In most books, however, not only does the author's name appear,

66

but other information is given about him. For example, his qualifications may be indicated on the dust-jacket and the other works he has written listed on the verso of the half-title page. Qualifications are most important with information books; an author's other works with imaginative literature. Of course, the qualifications need to be relevant ones, and his other writings preferably comparable ones.

If more information is needed about an author, several approaches can be tried in turn. First, find other books by the author to see if they reveal any further information about him. Second, look in biographical dictionaries listing authors, the *International authors' and writers' who's who*[1] being the outstanding work here. Third, look in biographical dictionaries to do with the subject field of the book, for example *Who's who in music* if it is a book on music, or ones which are otherwise appropriate, for instance, the *Academic who's who* with books of an academic nature.

Of course, with books that are not newly published, and especially with ones that have become classics or are at least by standard authors, there are a number of literary reference works that can be consulted, many of which add evaluative comments to the information they give. Such comments, incidentally, will more commonly be found about authors who are dead. Some of these reference books also include critical comments on the author's individual works. A survey of the major sources of evaluative information on books will be found in chapter 6.

Amongst the reference works about authors the following series are worthy of mention:

1 *Contemporary writers of the English language series* published in London by the St James Press. Novelists, poets, and dramatists are all covered in this series but the most useful volume is probably *Contemporary novelists*, the last edition of which was in 1976.

2 *Wilson authors' series* published in New York by the H W Wilson Company. There are many volumes in this series, some cover past centuries, others recent authors, for example *World authors, 1970-75*. Included in the Wilson series are several titles on children's writers such as the *Junior book of authors*, but the British publication *Twentieth century children's writers*[2] complements these titles.

3 *Oxford companion series*, which is not, of course, limited to literature, but which has several works giving information on books and authors, notably the *Oxford companion to English literature*[3] and the *Oxford companion to American literature*.[4]

The points that should be looked for in order to assess an author, the standing of whom is not already known, are: his education and qualifications; his experience and posts he has held (or holds); his subject knowledge and the school of thought within his subject field that he belongs to (if such schools exist); other works he has written (if any) and what type of books they are; and whether his publications have won any literary awards.[5] At the same time points relating to the research he has put into the writing of the book should be noted: what written sources has he used, what other people have helped him, what organizations has be contacted? Information on these points may be given by the author in his preface, or in a list of acknowledgements or in a list of sources.

With fictional writings and with some information books, particularly popular adult ones and those written for children, many of the points just listed are of less importance. Journalists rather than subject specialists often write the best popular adult information publications because they know how to write for a mass audience; whilst teachers sometimes write better children's information books than experts because of their knowledge of children.

Of course, in some books, there is no single author, or even two or three, but a large number of contributing writers. With these books the name of the editor is probably more significant than that of the authors, although it is also important to look carefully at all the information given about the contributors, and, if felt necessary, spot check them.

Editor etc The abbreviation 'etc' is added to the term editor in order to cover such people as advisers, revisers, translators, indexers and compilers. All these types of people should be looked for and investigated (if thought necessary) in the same way as it has been suggested authors should be considered and assessed. Some comments are called for on kinds of editors, in order to distinguish between title editors, series editors, and house or publishers' editors. The term title editor may be given to the person, who like the editor of a work with many contributors, is the all-important person behind the book. In the case of literary classics, the title editor is the person who has prepared the particular version of the classic including any introductory matter, critical notes, and special features. The series editor is the person, usually of some standing, who is reponsible for a particular publisher's series. His name will probably appear on the recto of the half-title page, but he may not act as much more than an adviser to the publisher

68

on the series. The house editor is the person within the publishing house made responsible for seeing the author's work through the press, and for ensuring that the publisher's house style[6] is followed. This kind of editor may also be responsible for the design of the publication. The name of the house editor is seldom given in a book, although it is occasionally found on the title page verso.

Artists and photographers In many information books the illustrations consist of ones that already exist, drawn together for the purposes of the publication from many sources and collections. However, in some information books and in most literary works they are, in whole or in part, commissioned for the book. In addition to the illustrations within the book, a commission for the design of the paper jacket may also be given. Some artists and photographers specialize in working on books, and certainly book illustrating does have its own particular needs. The names of artists and photographers most often appear on the verso of the title page, though if their contribution to the book is an important one, their names will appear on the title page. In some books, of course, such as children's picture books, the illustrator is more important than the author (indeed, often is the author). More information about book illustrators, if needed, may be found in *Who's who in art.*[7]

Designer Especially in more expensive and well-illustrated works, a book designer or typographer may be commissioned to ensure a high quality of layout and presentation, rather than the task left in the hands of the house editor. The designer's name will probably appear on the title page verso, and the appearance of such a name automatically suggests a book that has been carefully produced.

Printer etc As well as the name and address of the printer appearing in the book (either on the title page verso or in the colophon), the name of the binder, and even the name of the papermaker and the maker of the illustration blocks may appear. Usually the appearance of these other names suggests a book which has been produced to a high standard. Nowadays, books produced by a British publisher may be printed or bound in foreign countries rather than by British firms (the names of which are more likely to be known to and trusted by the evaluator). Large publishing organizations sometimes have their own printing establishments, and so the name of the printer is the same as the publisher's name.

Publisher The publisher is second only to the author in importance when it comes to considering the people connected with a book. There are a number of different kinds of publishers, and the evaluator will look to see which kind has been responsible for the issuing of the book, as it will affect his assessment of it.

First, there are trade publishers. Trade publishers are the well-known firms that publish the vast majority of the titles stocked by bookshops, firms such as Penguin Books, Andre Deutsch, and Faber and Faber. However, there are many small and less well-known firms in the publishing business, there are also firms that sell the books they publish by mail order rather than through bookshops. Many trade publishers specialize in publishing particular forms of books like paperbacks, or books in particular subject fields, such as Thames and Hudson, who specialize in the field of art. Some universities are trade rather than institutional publishers (see below), as they sell their books through normal trade channels.

Second, there are government publishers, together with those publishers who are responsible for the issue of publications of such bodies as the United Nations. Clearly, works issued by these publishers have an authority merely because they are official publications.

Third, there are institutional publishers. Most big institutions, societies, and similar organizations produce specialized and authoritative books appropriate to their field of interest, in the same way as does the Library Association.

The fourth kind is the individual who publishes his own book. Such publications are known as privately printed or published ones. Books of a local or specialized nature may have to be published in this way for economic reasons, but other privately published titles are usually of little value.

The privately published work should not be confused with the private press book. These books are produced by people or firms who are more concerned with the quality of production of their works than with their content matter. Private press publications will usually be of more interest to the book collector than to the librarian, but some libraries buy them. Private presses, like the famous Doves Press, were more a feature of the early twentieth century book world than they are of today's.

Lastly, the term semi-published needs to be defined. Librarians use this term to cover those publications that are produced basically for use within an institution or firm rather than for sale outside. For instance a library may produce and distribute to all its service points a staff manual in book form. Semi-published works often contain

70

valuable information, but it is not normally easy for librarians to trace and obtain them. Such titles may be considered part of what is now known as grey literature. This literature consists of those types of publications that are less widely disseminated and less readily available than most.

The name and address of the publisher, together with the place of publication, will appear on the title page leaf, and there will also usually appear any other addresses the publisher has in other countries. In addition, the names and addresses of overseas sales agents may be given. The kinds of books that publishers specialize in will be found in such publications as the *Writers' and artists' yearbook*,[8] and, of course, those titles a publisher issues within his speciality are given added authority by this. Works that are part of a publisher's series may also be considered to gain in authority for a similar reason. However, some series are of a very uneven quality and this probably particularly applies to children's information books. Sometimes a commercial publisher produces a work for a professional body or other reputable organization. Such publications obviously add the authority of the commissioning organization to that of the publisher. Professional organizations and official bodies that publish their own publications, of course, automatically give such publications authority merely by their names appearing on them.

The place of publication is generally of much less significance than the name of the publisher. However, it is important for the evaluator to know when a book is published abroad, as it will normally then emphasize a subject from the point of view of that country. A similar point to look out for is information (usually on the title page verso) to the effect that the book, though new to this country, has been previously published, sometimes under another title, by a foreign publisher.

Related to the place of publication is the subject of international publishing. A book published jointly by publishers from several countries can result in its being cheaper, but it may cause readers problems because its facts and its pictures can mean different things to people in different countries. If the publishers are from countries that do not have a common language, then the book will obviously have to be published with different language versions of its text. Its illustrations, however, will be common to all the versions.

Plan

Those criteria concerned with the plan of a publication form an important group, in that the whole book is likely to succeed or fail depending on whether it has been well planned in the first place. Fortunately, it is possible to find out about the plan of most information books just by looking at their preliminary matter, and indeed the titles of the majority of academic publications clearly sum it up.

Subject or theme The basic subject or theme of a book is obviously the most fundamental element in its plan, and so it is appropriate that it should be the first criterion here discussed. Though in information books of a serious nature the basic subject of the work is usually made clear by its title, in more popular information books, as the title is likely to be catchy rather than helpful, the evaluator will often have to examine contents pages or preface before being sure of a book's subject. In novels and other literary works, titles are also likely to be unhelpful, but the subject of such books is not significant in the same way as it is with information books. However, works of imaginative literature do commonly have a basic theme, and it is important that the evaluator finds out what this is. The blurb on the dust-jacket should give it when there is no preface or contents page. The word theme literally means (from the Greek) a topic put forward to be discussed. In other words it is the message or idea that the author is trying to put across to his readers. In fact, although it is in imaginative literature that themes are mostly to be found, for example the power of love, or the problem of suffering, such themes can also be found in books that are basically information books, but that try to put over a message or an idea as well as pure facts. In these books, therefore, it is not just subject or theme that has to be looked for, but both subject and theme.

Origins The origins of a book are how and why it came to be written. They are closely related to its aim and audience, and, like them, should be indicated in the book's preface. Probably they are less important in the evaluation of fiction than of information books, as imaginative works are basically the result of the author's creativity. An information book may originate, for example, from a teacher finding that no suitable book exists to which he can refer his pupils, and so he sets about writing such a book himself. This kind of origin would suggest that the book has been written to fill a definite need. Some other origins are less likely to result in a satisfactory book. For instance, a book may be no more than a series of lectures which are subsequently published, and so the publication was planned for another form of communication

72

than the book, and may not fit the book form successfully. As for books that arise out of radio and television programmes, they may or may not have acceptable origins. If they are planned to be used in connection with an educational programme, there can be no objection to them, but if they are only published to cash in on the popularity of, for example, a television series, they could well be much less satisfactory publications.

Obviously, the origins of books which are not being published for the first time but are just further editions can concern the evaluator less, as the book would not have reached a subsequent edition if it had completely failed to meet some need. On the other hand, books which have been published before, but not in the version in which they are now published, the evaluator should basically treat as new publications. Examples of works taking such forms are abridged versions of books, and foreign language works in new translations.

Aim The aim, object or purpose of a book is obviously important, and indeed may result in the book being the overall type of work it is, such as textbook or monograph. The aim should be clearly defined in the preface (if there is one). An author who does not declare his aim is worthy of censure. At the end of the evaluator's examination of a book, the subject of aim needs to be returned to and the question asked: does the publication succeed in its aim? The aim of a book is obviously closely related to the readers or audience for which it has been written. The book's aim is also related to how its readers will use it. For example, a children's encyclopaedia will aim to provide material for quick-reference and perhaps for browsing, but not for reading from cover to cover.

Audience Like the aim of a book, its audience should be precisely defined in the preface of the publication. A publisher may try to suggest in his publicity material that a particular book will suit many needs, but it is usually only really relevant to the needs of just one sort of person. Typical audiences are children (usually of a particular age group), students of one kind or another, subject specialists, and, of course, the general public. When a work has been examined the question that must be asked is: does the book serve satisfactorily the audience for which it has been designed?

Variant issues An issue of a book is that part of an edition or impression produced by the publisher in a particular form. For instance, a book may be issued both in hardback and paperback. Some publications have variant issues in which the contents differ, for instance

73

Whitaker's almanack is issued in a shorter version which omits the last few hundred pages of the overall contents. Variant issues should be indicated on the title page verso. Their existence usually indicates that the work has a variety of potential purchasers, and the publisher is trying to appeal to as many of them as possible.

Special services This criterion will only apply to a very small number of books, but, for example, an encyclopaedia publisher sometimes offers a special service in the form of an enquiry bureau, and purchasers of the encyclopaedia may contact the bureau when they want to know something which they cannot find in the encyclopaedia itself. Occasionally the availability of a special service is wider than buyers of the published book, as with the Benn's Editorial Media Information Service (**BEMIS**), which service is not restricted to purchasers of *Benn's press directory*.

A special service, as outlined above, needs to be distinguished from the service form of publishing information. This is the publication of printed information, not in book form, but in a leaflet or slip format. The information is so sold that the purchaser can buy only part of the service if he wants. For example, the *Extel British company service* offers information about British firms in this form, unlike the *Stock Exchange official yearbook* which offers similar information but in conventional book form. Incidentally, publishers of services of this kind are increasingly making them available not just on paper but via screen-based information systems, that is, through television set based viewdata systems such as the British Telecom's *Prestel*, and through on-line computer terminal systems such as the *Dialog* one from the American firm of Lockheed.[9]

Related works Many books are related to other books, normally also ones put out by the same publisher. The most obvious type of related work is the new edition, which is clearly related to the work's earlier editions. Similar to this relationship is that of the work based on a previously published book, as, for example, the *Shorter Oxford English dictionary* based on the main *Oxford English dictionary*. A third type of relationship is that between the titles comprising a publisher's series. All types of related works should be mentioned in a book's preliminaries, and their existence commonly adds to the work's authority.

Contents

The criteria which come under this heading are dealt with, as has already been mentioned, in the next chapter. Although a few of the criteria within this heading can be applied to books of all kinds, basically the ones that relate to fiction (and other imaginative literature) are different from those that relate to information books. The criteria for fiction concern matters such as plot and characterization, whilst those for information books are concerned with matters like accuracy and up-to-dateness.

In the next chapter, in addition to separate sections on fiction and information books, short sections with additional comments will be found on some categories of these publications. At the end of the section on information books there are ones on children's information books, and on quick-reference books. At the end of the section on fiction there are ones on children's fiction (divided into story books and picture books), and other imaginative literature (divided into plays and poetry).

Organization

The criteria under this heading are obviously more important in information books than in imaginative literature, in that information books need to put over their contents in a well-organized and easily understood way, and also need to allow readers to find quickly any piece of information that they contain.

Arrangement Most books, other than quick-reference books, are arranged by chapters, though sometimes the chapters themselves are grouped into broader units, usually called parts. In literary works, of course, the arrangement is partly determined by literary form. For example, a play will be arranged by act and scene. The order of the main sequence of the text of a book should be logical, understandable, and be appropriate to the plan of the work. It should be complemented by additional or supplementary sequences where these are necessary.

It will, of course, be obvious from a book's contents page (if it has one) how a book is arranged, but more detailed matters of arrangement, such as what type of alphabetization[10] is used in an alphabetically arranged information book, can only be appreciated by examining the textmatter.

Contents list etc The provision of a list of contents and a list of illustrations in the preliminary matter of a book is part of its organization, so is the provision made in some information books for the sections of each chapter to be listed at the beginning of it. The evaluator should look to see what lists are provided, how detailed they are, and, in the case of the list of illustrations, how complete.

Indexes Alphabetically arranged books are usually self-indexing, as is a typical dictionary, but most other information books need to be indexed (though literary works seldom need to be). Indeed, several indexes may be provided in an information book; for example an index of people (eg authors), an index of places, and an index of subjects. The evaluator should not only look to see what indexes are provided, he should assess whether they are easy to use, comprehensive, accurate, consistent in the information they give, and precise in their references. For instance, in a book printed with two-columned pages, the index entries should refer to columns and not just pages. He should also look to see if there are cross-references within the index, if the book's illustrations are indexed, and if, when there are several references under a particular entry, whether the main reference is indicated in any way.

The indexing of books is being taken increasingly seriously and certainly it needs to be. Indicative of this is the annual award, the Wheatley medal, now made by the Library Association and the Society of Indexers for the best index of the year.

Cross-references These are especially a feature of self-indexing quick-reference books like encyclopaedias. However, an author of an information book arranged by chapters should also use cross-references within his chapters. There are two types of cross-references, *see* references, which indicate where to look when the wrong place or heading has been tried, and *see also* references, which indicate where further relevant information may be found.

Headings There is a need, at least in most information books, for further headings and sub-headings in addition to the main chapter headings. These make books easier to refer to, easier to browse through, and add to their legibility. The evaluator should ask the questions: what use is made of headings and sub-headings; and are the headings systematically numbered in any way? Related to the use of headings is the use of extra space between some paragraphs. In works of fiction this is often the only way in which a new section of the narrative is indicated.

Design
This group of criteria is probably more important in the average book than is generally realized, for good design is basically unobtrusive. Certainly, the pleasure of reading a literary work, as well as the efficient use of an information book, are affected by how well the publication's contents are presented by its designer (or typographer, as

a book designer is more properly called). A good guide to book design is Ruari McLean's *The Thames and Hudson manual of typography*.[11]

To some extent, the criteria dealt with here, and those just examined under the heading of Organization have a complementary purpose, for both sets of criteria are concerned with enabling readers to find their way as effectively as possible through the book's contents. The heading of Design is also complementary to Book production, as it is only when design and production are considered together that the overall look, feel (and some would add smell) of the book can be assessed.

Format The size and shape of books cause problems to librarians because unusually shaped ones, for example, books in a landscape format (that is, wider than they are high) will not easily fit on library shelves. However, a book's size and shape is determined, quite reasonably, not by librarians' wishes, but by the subject and contents of the book. For instance, art books tend to be larger than the average book, so that large illustrations of paintings and other works of art can be included. But the type of book that probably has the greatest variety of formats, the better to put over its contents, is the children's picture book. The design and format of these books may indeed include such unusual features as pages of different sizes and even ones with holes in (as in Eric Carle's *The very hungry caterpillar*).

Layout Once the designer of a book has decided on its format, he can plan the layout of its contents. This is a job which may take some time, especially in profusely illustrated works. The layout of a book is particularly concerned with its margins, the placing of both its text-matter and its illustrations, and with any purely decorative features that are included.

Legibility It is the author who makes a book readable, but it is the typographer who makes it legible. His greatest problem is probably designing cheap reprints of books where, to cut costs, the size of the book and so the size of the type used has to be on the small side. But legibility is affected not just by type size and style, but by such factors as the colour of paper, the amount of space between the lines of type, and the length of the lines. In children's books, especially those for younger children, it is normal to aim at a higher level of legibility than in adult books. An exception is, of course, those large-print versions of works designed for those with poor eyesight. The best introduction to the subject of legibility is Herbert Spencer's *The visible word*.[12]

Aesthetic aspects Even in information books, aesthetic aspects of book design are relevant, but such aspects are admittedly more relevant

77

to, for example, de-luxe editions of the classics. Aesthetic aspects of design are not hard to identify, though it may be hard to explain fully why one book's design is more aesthetically pleasing than another's. Aesthetic aspects include the harmony of text and illustrations, the use of colour, the use of space, and the establishing of pleasing proportions.

Production

A well-designed book is usually a well-produced one. The criteria that concern how a book is made may not be particularly important ones to the average reader, but to the librarian, as well as to the book collector, they are criteria that merit careful consideration. Both librarians and book collectors seek the knowledge that will allow them to appreciate the finer points of the craft of book-making, and also seek to be aware of the recommendations of the British Standards Institution and of similar bodies on book production.[13] Peter New's *Book production*[14] is designed as an introduction to this topic for librarians.

Methods The methods used in book production include those that result in books being illustrated by particular processes, and being bound in a certain way. The correct choice of illustration processes is especially relevant to books containing reproductions of paintings. It can only be assessed, however, by an evaluator with knowledge of such processes. Binding methods, on the other hand, can be assessed with less specialized knowledge. If, for instance, the binding is so tight it does not allow the book to lie flat when opened, it is obviously at fault. For the librarian, of course, many modern methods of binding, such as the spiral variety, cause shelving problems, whilst books whose pages are kept together using a loose-leaf method of binding are likely to have some of their pages go missing.

Craftmanship Though book production today is carried out by machine not by hand, the term craftmanship is still the most appropriate one for this criterion. Poor craftmanship results in such things as the faulty inking of pages, and the omission or misplacing of groups of pages when the book is bound.

Materials Most books in libraries receive heavy use, and so need both paper and binding which will withstand such use. The larger the book, the greater the strength of the materials needed. However, strong materials are also needed for children's picture books as, although these contain a comparatively small number of pages, they have to stand up to being knocked about. But good quality materials are not just strong materials, they are aesthetically pleasing ones. The choice of materials for a particular book should bear this in mind. Overall, the materials chosen should be appropriate; the average book cannot be expected to be made like a collector's item.

Placing

This final group of criteria is the one in which the findings of the evaluation so far are summarized and the evaluator's conclusions reached. Student librarians may find, because of their lack of experience and limited knowledge, that the criteria under this headings are the ones on which it is hardest for them to make a judgement.

Price The price of a book should be reasonable compared with similar publications. However, it should be remembered that it is the number of copies of a book which can be sold that mainly determines price, not factors like number of pages. Therefore, even small books on specialized subjects can be relatively expensive. Of course, second-hand copies of most books can be obtained much more cheaply than new ones, but the reduction in price has to be paid for by a reduction in the quality of the book's physical condition. Increasingly, however, books in mint condition are becoming available as remainders[15] quite soon after their original publication date, and at a cost no more than may be paid for second-hand copies. Books in mint condition can also, of course, be obtained at reduced prices from book clubs by those who are members, although book clubs have to work within certain agreed sale and price practices.

The sale of books in this country is controlled by the Net Book Agreement, which means that booksellers cannot normally sell books at lower than the price fixed by the publisher. However, a few books, mainly school textbooks, are outside this agreement, and so are described as non-net. The reason for their being treated differently is because they are produced to be sold in bulk through special educational suppliers to education authorities.

Comparisons There are four main kinds of comparisons that can be carried out to help assess where a book should be placed. They are: comparisons with past or alternative editions of the same book; comparisons with variant issues of the same edition; comparisons with books having similar aims and containing similar contents; and comparisons with alternative sources of similar material, such as computer-based on-line information services. There is also a fifth comparison that library book selectors have to carry out. It is the comparison of the work under evaluation with any similar titles that the library already has in stock.

The making of comparisons is relevant to all kinds of books, but with literary classics the emphasis needs to be rather different, being on comparing the editions put out by different publishers. Some will differ from others only in quality of design and production, but others are likely to contain different editorial information and notes, and indeed may contain a different version of the text.

Uniqueness After the comparisons have been completed, the evaluator can ask certain questions about the uniqueness of the work. With information books, they are: does the book contain new information, or does it present old information in a new way? If it does either of these things, it can be considered to justify its existence and to possess a certain uniqueness. With fiction and other imaginative literature, the question to be asked is: does the book have originality, or, at the very least, does it cast new light on old truths? If it does, it is likely to be a worthwhile addition to literature.

Quality A book measuring up well to the criteria put forward so far can be considered to have pased the main test of quality. But an additional test of quality may be made. Admittedly, it is perhaps more applicable to the average reader than to the average evaluator. It is whether it is felt that the time spent reading the work was worthwhile. Of course, most publications have both strengths and weaknesses, and so a good quality book is not the same thing as a perfect one. Incidentally, a book of high quality will also usually have considerable influence and at the same time be well used.

Usefulness A book of high quality may be, surprisingly enough, a work of very limited usefulness, there being just no demand for it. The evaluator needs to ask two questions relating to usefulness. They are: does the book fill a need, and will it be read? If the evaluator is not just assessing the book but also considering purchasing it, he will obviously add a third question: is it worth buying? He may indeed, in a library situation, ask a fourth question: has there already been any positive demand from library users for the book? For instance, they may have filled in book request forms for the title. However, as was commented on in the preface to this book, there are many factors other than those that directly relate to the placing of the title by the library evaluator that determine whether it will be purchased by his library. These factors are mainly administrative ones such as the library's book selection policy. They are factors geared essentially, in fact, to the nature and organization of the library.

Notes and references

1 *International authors' and writers' who's who, 1981* 9th ed. Ely, Melrose Press, 1981.

2 Kirkpatrick, D L, ed. *Twentieth century children's writers* London, Macmillan, 1978.

3 *Oxford companion to English literature* 4th ed. Oxford, Clarendon Press, 1967.

4 *Oxford companion to American literature* 4th ed. New York, Oxford University Press, 1965.

5 Weber, O S and Calvert, S J *Literary and library prizes* 10th ed. New York, Bowker, 1980. This is the best work to consult on the subject, having an author index.

6 House style is to do with those minor aspects of writing and printing like hyphenation, spelling, and the use of capital letters. It may also cover rules concerning the design aspects of books. Publishers sometimes issue authors with a guide to their house style. Some of the publications of the British Standards Institution are also designed to aid in this area. The relevant ones will be found listed in the Institution's publication Sectional List SL 35 *Documentation (including UDC): standards for the editor, publisher, librarian and information scientist* (September 1978).

7 *Who's who in art* 19th ed. Havant, Art Trade Press, 1979.

8 *Writers' and artists' yearbook, 1981* London, Black, 1981.

9 The evaluation of these information systems is outside the scope of this book, but the librarian needs to know how to assess them. An introduction to their evaluation will be found in Rowley, J E and Turner, C M D *Dissemination of information* (London, Deutsch, 1978, Section 6.3) This introduction forms part of a chapter entitled 'External information services', the name often given to published information services as opposed to reader services of an information nature offered by individual libraries.

10 There are two main types of alphabetization, word-by-word (ie New Zealand before Newfoundland) and letter-by-letter (ie Newfoundland before New Zealand).

11 McLean, R *The Thames and Hudson manual of typography* London, Thames and Hudson, 1980.

12 Spencer, H *The visible word* London, Lund Humphries, 1969.

13 Sectional List SL 22 of the British Standards Institution *Printing and stationery, paper and board* (September 1979) is the one that covers their book production publications.

14 New, P *Book production* London, Bingley/Saur, 1979.

15 Remainders are copies of books in new condition sold off at a cheaper price by publishers when they look like being left on their hands.

Chapter 5

SPECIALIZED CRITERIA – CONTENTS

The criteria covered by this chapter, it was made clear in the last, are those that come under the heading Contents. They are entitled specialized criteria because they are not the same for all kinds of books, but differ depending as to whether it is an information book or a work of imaginative literature that is under evaluation. The two main sections of this chapter deal respectively with information books and with fiction.

Although each of these sections is followed by the assessment of certain narrower forms of publications, for example reference books, these forms are not dealt with in detail, but rather those particular points that are especially relevant to them are selected for attention. Nor does this chapter cover the additional criteria that affect the assessment of books in particular subject fields. For guidance here, works on subject librarianship should be consulted, but Broadus' *Selecting material for libraries*[1] is also worth consulting as it looks separately at most subject fields.

When appraising an individual title, the evaluator, in addition to choosing the appropriate set of criteria from this chapter, must obviously use the criteria in the last. A quick-reference list of the criteria from both chapters relevant to information books and to fiction, respectively, will be found in the Appendix.

If the two sets of criteria that are looked at in this chapter are compared, it will suggest to the evaluator some of the reasons why a different set is needed for information books than for fiction and other imaginative works. It may also make the evaluator realize that information books are more definitively evaluated, even though the critics pay less attention to them than to imaginative literature. Imaginative works are harder to assess objectively; they have to be read right through, and call for real empathy on the part of the critic. It could be argued, perhaps, that novels are reviewed as often as they are because they have a longer potential life than information books, but it is more likely that they are popular with reviewers because they may be read by a wide audience, have aims that are more literary, and allow the reviewers quite legitimately to disagree with each other.

The evaluator, no matter what kind of work he is assessing, should obviously consider it worthy of serious attention, though he may reasonably examine an important publication at greater length. He should also quite clearly, when he has to assess controversial publications, be as impartial as possible. The general principle in library book selection as regards controversial works is that no book should be excluded from the stock of a library merely because its contents are controversial, and that any censorship should be limited to that established by the law of the land. Censorship is obviously applicable, though not necessarily for the same reasons, to children's books as well as adult ones. However, there is a further difficulty that relates to the censoring of these: the adult is not able to see them with a child's eye, and so may therefore censor unnecessarily.

Information books
This section is concerned with the detailed evaluation of the contents of books whose primary purpose is to inform or educate. Most books published are information books of one kind or another. Though the majority of the criteria here put forward can be applied to all of them, it will be found that a few of the criteria are not applicable to certain publications. As might be expected, which criteria are applicable and which are not in any particular case depends on the nature and subject of the book. Considered later will be two important kinds of information books, children's information books and quick-reference publications.

The contents of information books have many facets, and so there are a good many criteria to be examined (twenty in all). Some of these are more efficiently dealt with if the evaluator has subject knowledge, and so it is probably the contents group of criteria that causes the most problems to the librarian who is not a subject specialist in the field covered by the book, even though he is an experienced book selector. When examining a book's contents, the evaluator should look not only to see how they measure up to the individual criteria, but also if they are appropriate to the overall plan of the book, and are consistent with the claims made for the book in its preface and in the publicity put out about it.

84

Standing The first edition of a work has no standing other than that of the people behind it. But a book with a previous edition does have, as it can be considered that its contents would not have been revised had they been of low quality. The standing of a book is most clearly indicated by its bibliographical history as given on the title page verso.

Research: methods and sources The authority of a work also depends on the sources and methods used by the author in the preparation of the publication. The sources and methods used should be given clearly, either in the preliminary or the subsidiary pages, and also revealed by the notes and references given throughout the textmatter. Examining the sources and methods will show the scholarship of the book and suggest its trustworthiness and its orginality. It must be admitted, however, that unless the evaluator is an expert in particular research methods, for example statistical ones, he will not be able to assess precisely the validity of those used. Authors who go to original manuscript material and other primary sources, who carry out observations and investigations of their own, and who are prepared to reveal fully their research methods, are the ones who can be considered to be most trustworthy.

Soundness The soundness of a book's contents is whether the statements made by the author, and particularly the comments he gives and the conclusions he draws, follow from the facts he has presented. If the evaluator is not sure about how to find flaws in an author's argument, he should consult works such as *Straight and crooked thinking*.[2] Authority and soundness go together, but an author may use good information sources, and then draw unsound judgements from the evidence they offer him. (Of course, his textmatter may also be unsound because of the use of poor or insufficient sources.)

Length Looking at the length of a book obviously tells the evaluator something about its contents. It may also suggest to him that the book's length is artificial: for example, a publication which is part of a publisher's series may have to be of a standard length, the whole series having the same number of pages. Such a publisher's policy may enable the price of all the titles in the series to be identical, but it is likely to result in subjects being dealt with in fewer or more pages than are really needed.

Scope The scope of a book is its range or breadth. No one work can really cover the whole of knowledge, and so authors place limitations on the scope of their publications. Not only do they lay down subject boundaries, they may limit themselves in other ways, for example by covering their subject only in so much as it relates to one particular country or one historical period. The scope of a book should be indicated both by its preface and by its contents page. Generally speaking, the higher the intellectual level of a book, the more narrow will be its scope. The scope of a book should be appropriate to its plan, and the limitations that the author places thereon should be reasonable ones. The field that the book states it covers should correspond with its actual textmatter, and this textmatter should not have any subject gaps in it.

Detail The detail of a book is complementary to its scope; that is, it is an indication of the depth and comprehensiveness of the book's contents. In the average book it is not so clearly indicated by its preface and contents page as is its scope, and the textmatter will have to be examined before the precise amount of detail in the book can be determined. On the whole, the higher the intellectual level of a book, the more detailed will be the coverage of its subject. A book claiming comprehensiveness in its coverage should indeed be that. Generally, a book should have the amount and kind of detail that it claims to have and which suit its plan. There is nothing wrong in a book dealing selectively with the subjects that fall within its scope, indeed most books have to, but it should select its material carefully to give appropriate depth of coverage.

Viewpoint The scope and coverage of a book will be partly determined by the viewpoint that the author has or decides to take on his subject. For example, he may set out to try and prove a particular theory, and so take an appropriate viewpoint to help him do this. Alternatively, he may take the viewpoint of a particular school of thought, because he belongs to that school of thought, and this too will result in his book dealing with its subject from a certain angle. Again, he may want to approach his subject in a way that will emphasize a particular aspect of it, for example its historical aspect or its philosophical aspect. The way that a book is angled towards its subject may not always be clear (be wary of the author who is not prepared to make it clear) but reading the preface and sampling the text, together with finding out something about the author, should reveal it.

Bias Clearly the quality of a book will be affected if its contents are biased. If a book deals unfairly with some of the topics covered by it, or the author shows prejudice in some of his comments and conclusions, it may be unacceptably biased. Bias is more acceptable when it is obvious, for instance, the result of the viewpoint taken: for

86

example, one would not expect a Roman Catholic book on the papacy to cover its subject in the same way as a Protestant one. However, bias is often not obvious, and it is only when the book is carefully read that the author's religious, political, racist, or other prejudices come to light.

Balance A publication may be unbiased and yet still unbalanced: for example, a history of England may devote too much space to the pre-Norman period. There are various reasons for unbalanced publications. For instance, it has been known for the publishers of a multi-volumed quick-reference book to run short of money, and so perhaps have to cover the letters M-Z in one volume, whilst having devoted six volumes to the letters A-L. Even in a less unbalanced publication, it is possible to see two subjects of equal importance treated with unequal length. The cause of this may be just that, with a book that has a number of contributors, one of them wrote much more than he was asked. It can be seen then that although bias and lack of balance are related, the former is basically the result of personal attitudes and prejudices, whilst the latter is caused more by bad management.

Level This is the last of the criteria particularly related to the author's selection of his contents. The intellectual level of the contents of a book is clearly related to its plan. Levels are most easily recognized in textbooks where the title of the work often states that it is elementary, intermediate or advanced. Level can be judged from the author's style and choice of language; the lower the level, the simpler will be both style and language. The level will also affect the material that the author decides to include in his work. Level may be mentioned in the book's preface, but it will be necessary to dip into its text pages to check on it properly. At the end of examining the book, the evaluator should ask the question: is the level of the book's contents consistent with its professed aim and audience?

Style The author's style in an information book is less important than it is in a work of literature, but it is still a criterion to be considered. It is especially important in those information books not written for subject specialists, and in those that have been translated from a foreign language, as in the latter the original author's style and indeed sense may not be satisfactorily conveyed by the translator.

The style that an information book is written in should be first of all suitable for the publication's audience. Second, it should be clear and efficient, rather than literary or poetic. Third, it should be, as far as possible, interesting. The success of an author's style can be seen particularly in the way he deals with explaining technical processes or other difficult concepts.

Accuracy Accuracy is essential in information books for even the odd inaccuracy in such works is misleading and may be disastrous. Inaccuracies result from many causes, for example poor sources, poor editing and poor proof reading. Dates, addresses and statistics are places where inaccuracies often occur and such inaccuracies can frequently be spotted without much difficulty.

Up-to-dateness Accuracy and up-to-dateness go together. Especially with books on science and technology and with those on current affairs, the problem of having as up-to-date information as possible in the contents matter is a very real one. Normally, it takes more than a year for a major work to go through all the stages of being published, and so it is actually impossible to have such a book really up-to-date. The up-to-dateness of the contents of a book can be most effectively checked by looking, not at the book's publication date or even at its copyright date, but by searching for the latest dates that can be found in its text and in its bibliographical information. Lack of up-to-dateness, of course, cannot only be found in individual facts and figures, but also in other aspects of the book's contents. The evaluator should therefore ask the questions: are the latest developments in the work's subject field dealt with, and is the author up to date in his ideas and receptive to the latest ideas of others?

Revision A distinction needs to be drawn between minor and major revision. Minor revision of a book is the issuing of corrections and similar updating procedures, like the inclusion of a supplement in a work's end-matter. Minor revision measures do not cost much, but do not result in much overall change in the contents of a book. Major revision is costly, but is also much more thorough. The usual way of carrying out major revision is to publish a new edition, though other methods may be used especially with quick-reference books (see pp92-3).

The evaluator should check books to see if minor revision has been incorporated into them. He should then examine the subject of major revision by turning to the preface of the work. With a first edition, he should look for any mention of a programme of future updating. With works that are in their second or subsequent editions, he should check the title page verso to see how frequently they have been revised during their publishing history. The problem of all revision is for the publisher a financial one, as he wants the money spent on revision to be more than recouped from additional sales.

Permanence It a book's contents are regularly revised they clearly become of longer lasting value. The relative permanence of an information book's contents is otherwise most determined by the subject of the book, some subjects dating more quickly than others. The contents of information books that have become classics may be judged the most enduring; the contents of those written about matters of the moment the most ephemeral. The evaluator should remember that the book's authorship is another factor affecting its permanence, an author of standing making for a work of greater permanence.

Bibliographical information This criterion, together with the next three, relate to specialized aspects of a book's contents. Bibliographical information is of especial interest to librarians as they are experts on the subject, and three types of this information may be differentiated. First, there are lists of sources used by the author (discussed earlier in this chapter). Second, a type overlapping the first, there are bibliographical references, which give, for example, details of publications from which the author has quoted. These need to be sufficiently detailed and precise to be fully identifiable, and also consistent, accurate and up to date. The third type of this information takes the form of bibliographies, reading lists, and guides to further study. This should have the same qualities as bibliographical references and, in addition, be well selected and whenever possible briefly annotated.

Visual information The term visual information covers the wide variety of illustrative or graphic information found in information books. As well as diagrams and pictures of all kinds, there can be flow-charts, graphs, maps and scale drawings. In some information books, such as those on geography, visual information is clearly especially important, and the evaluator needs to recognize its importance. The overall value of visual material is that it can communicate information that cannot, or cannot easily, be put into words. Many questions may be asked by the evaluator about a book's visual information, chief of which are: what sort of visuals are there?; is all the visual information needed?; should more visual information have been provided?; are the types of visuals used the right types to serve the purposes of the book?; have the visuals been specially designed for the book?; are the visuals of a reasonable quality?; are they placed near to the textmatter they are supposed to support?; is use made of colour?; are captions always given?; are they clear?; are the visuals fully listed in the list of illustrations?

With particular kinds of visual information even more questions may

89

need to be asked. For instance, with maps, the evaluator will usually ask such questions as: has the right kind of scale been chosen?; how easy is it to locate places?; what keys are there for identifying the colours and signs used on the maps?

Special features The term special features is one that may be used to mean any comparatively unusual features of a book, which aim to give it extra value. For example, a publication that includes a glossary may claim it a special feature. Some kinds of information books are more likely to have special features than others; for instance textbooks tend to have such special features as chapter summaries and sample examination questions. Although most special features genuinely aid readers, the evaluator should be on the lookout for ones that are little more than a gimmick.

Supporting material This material is so called because it does not form part of the main textmatter of the book, but rather supports it. It is of two main kinds, first, notes such as footnotes (normally printed in smaller type to show it is supporting material) and, second, appendices. The main purpose of notes is to provide background information on points made in the main text, and in some scholarly books such notes are both copious and of great value. Appendices supplement the text by giving longer pieces of supporting material. The evaluator needs to note the extent of any supporting material, and try and assess how much it will help those readers who wish to use it.

Effect The last criterion for information books is more subjective than the others — it is the effect reading the book has had on the evaluator. Even information books can have a powerful effect on readers[4] as, although such books are not usually written to appeal to their readers' emotions, many of them do stimulate, challenge, convince, and even move. Some information books, therefore, may be criticized if they leave the reader cold, whilst all information books that made him want to read more on the subject, or make him think again about views he has previously held, are to be praised. One more point, the evaluator should look to see if the author states in his preface that he wants his book to affect its readers in a certain way. If he does, the question can be asked: has be succeeded?

Children's information books
Perhaps the most obvious difference between the contents of books written for adults and those written for children is that the latter (fiction as well as non-fiction) must pay more attention to the age of

90

the reader they are aimed at, and to his reading ability. The criterion of level, of which readability is a part, is an important one with children's works. The choice of words, the length of words, the length and complexity of sentences, are amongst the factors that affect the level of readability. But also affecting it are the ideas and concepts used by the author, and the degree of abstractness of the contents. It is possible using readability formulae, which measure factors such as the above, to test the readability level of any book or other piece of writing roughly and see that it is appropriate. The book by Gilliland, *Readability* (already mentioned on page 64) is as useful as any for suggesting appropriate formulae and procedures.

But the style of children's information books cannot be judged solely on whether it is in accord with accepted readability formulae. It needs to show insight and enthusiasm. The author should reveal such insight into the child's mind that the child feels personally involved with the subject he is reading about, and the author should show such enthusiasm in his writing that he stimulates similar enthusiasm in the child. It has been suggested that authors of children's information books should educate their readers rather than just put over pure information. This may be disputed, but certainly they should enthuse as well as inform.

However, though the textmatter of all children's books must be appropriately written, increasingly children's information books put over their information by means of pictures. Indeed, with some information books the words of the author are very much secondary. With works for younger children drawings rather than photographs are the rule, as they can be made simple and clear. For children of all ages coloured illustrations have an added attraction, though they are more expensive to print. The evaluator must spend some time weighing up the quality and value of the illustrations and other visual material. He needs to beware of those publications that at first sight impress; but when examined more closely prove to be no more than superficially attractive, the illustrations being in fact of little use.

Undoubtedly, well-illustrated works appeal to children and it is often the illustrations that draw a child to a particular title rather than to any other work on the subject. Also appealing to children is finding, having used the book, that it incorporates special features which enable him to follow up what he has read and further the interest that has been aroused by the reading. Such features include games, puzzles and

91

practical activities. The last sort of feature is obviously appropriate for books on subjects like nature study. It is also appropriate for information books that are being used as school textbooks, and in schools today, especially because of the emphasis on project work, formal textbooks have to a large extent been replaced by information books that are produced not just for class use in schools but for sale to homes and libraries.

It is to be remembered that the bibliographical features of a book are another place to which a child can turn when wanting to follow up what he has read. Children's information books should therefore include some suggestions for further reading which have been carefully selected and which are books that are easily obtainable.

Quick-reference books

Quick-reference books are designed to be dipped into rather than read from cover to cover, and their contents reflect this. They are an important category of book for librarians because of their value in reader service. They are also books that librarians select with care as they are often expensive publications, especially when multi-volumed. Such multi-volumed works are the ones that have the most difficulty keeping up to date as the revision process is for them so great a task. Therefore, the publishers of such works, especially encyclopaedia publishers, have tried to find alternative means of revising books other than the traditional method of compiling new editions. Evaluators should look to see what revision method (or combination of methods) has been adopted by the publishers of a quick-reference book. He will probably come across the following alternatives to new editions: continuous revision; publication of a volume or a part at a time; loose-leaf format; supplementary volumes; and yearbooks.

The method of updating known as continuous revision has become fairly popular. It is a method that results in the work being constantly revised and frequently printed, often annually. Continuous revision, if carried out thoroughly, is a sound method, even though it leaves the book selector with the problem of wondering when to buy another copy, as the revision carried out each year is likely to be too little to justify the annual purchase of the work.

The revision of a publication a volume or part at a time does not cause the book selector the same problem but it does result in another problem, this time one relating to using the work. It is that the publication's contents will vary in their up-to-dateness from one volume or

92

part to another.

The use of a loose-leaf format is a method seldom used for revision purposes except in certain subject areas such as law, where up-to-dateness is crucial. It has the advantage that just small sections of the text can be updated and issued whenever necessary, but, quite apart from the disadvantage that pages may be more easily lost, it has been found that the purchasers of loose-leaf publications are reluctant to insert any revised pages they receive.

The last two revision methods, supplements and yearbooks, are not in fact ways of revising a complete work, but they are commonly used ways of keeping one up to date between complete revisions. Supplements may be either regular or irregular. They are useful, but they force readers to look in an extra place every time they require information, and, of course, they are of little use without the main work. Yearbooks, on the other hand, are usually more independent publications, but because of this, are less directly relevant to the needs of the users of the main work.

Quick-reference books need to be systematically revised; they are also expected to be as unbiased as possible. The evaluator should look to see if he can find any statement by the compiler as to how the work tries to be fair to every point of view. For example, it has been known for an encyclopaedia to devote two articles rather than one to a controversial topic so that the two opposing viewpoints on it may both be given a fair hearing.

An encyclopaedia with the above policy might well consider it to be a special feature of the book, but frequently in quick-reference works a special feature is one that normally belongs to a different type of quick-reference book. For instance a dictionary may be given an atlas feature. Such special features librarians look upon with suspicion, as they prefer a reference book that keeps to its main purpose to one that also tries to serve a second. They feel the work may well end up serving neither satisfactorily.

The evaluation of individual types of quick-reference books is usually covered in textbooks on reference materials, but probably the best guidance will be found in the American Library Association's Subscription Books' Committee *Manual*. [3]

Fiction

Although the emphasis in this section is on the evaluation of prose fiction, that is, novels, short stories and miscellaneous items such as published collections of jokes, the evaluation of poetry and drama, as well as children's story books and picture books, is given separate consideration later. There is no attempt in this section to distinguish at all between different kinds of fictional writings. However, it is common to pigeon-hole light or popular fiction publications into a limited number of categories (often called genres), and assume that a work, because it belongs to a particular genre, will have particular strengths and weaknesses. The main such categories are (in alphabetical order): Country, Detective, Family, Historical, Horror, Humour, Romance, Science fiction, Sea, Sport, Spy, Supernatural, Thriller, War, and Western. In addition, a few other groups may be distinguished, for example novels for teenagers and ones aimed at adults still learning how to read. It would be wrong for the evaluator to try to over-categorize popular fiction works he examines, for many cut across the named categories, just as much as it would be wrong for him to assume automatically that strengths and weaknesses of a particular genre apply to every title within that genre.

There are seventeen criteria that will help aid the evaluation of fiction. Obviously, these criteria need to be applied rather differently to works of a literary nature than to those fictional works whose main aim is to entertain. The evaluator should also bear in mind that, compared with information books, the evaluation of fiction is a more subjective process as works of fiction essentially convey an experience. The application of objective standards to them leads then to somewhat less successful results than with information books. There is no doubt that student librarians may also find the evaluation of fiction difficult because they have not read widely enough, and especially not read enough literary classics. They may, therefore, have to turn more to the opinions of reviewers and critics and draw on their greater knowledge and experience than when evaluating information books. A third reason why they may find the evaluation of fiction more difficult is because, as a rule, fiction titles have little in the way of helpful information in either their preliminary pages or end-matter. This means that, short of giving the work what was called in chapter 3 a Full Examination, it is very hard to assess a fiction title satisfactorily.

The criteria now examined are set out in as logical an order as possible, and they are also arranged as closely as possible to the criteria already given in this chapter for information books.

Standing The reputation and standing of works of classical fiction is obvious; the standing of more popular publications of the past is

94

less clear, but it nevertheless exists. Newly published fiction has no standing as such (other than that of its author and publisher), unless it has already been published in another form, for example in a magazine. However, with fictional works, when the author has already had published other stories with the same hero, or ones to which the present story is a sequel, then this automatically gives the new work some initial standing. Titles, when published in paperback form, usually have some standing, as the majority of paperbacks are issued because of a previously successful hardback. The bibliographical history of fictional works tends to be less fully given on the title page verso than in information books, but examining it may help establish a title's standing.

Research: methods and sources This criterion, like the next two, concerns the raw material out of which the author fashions his work. It is a criterion easily overlooked when fiction is being evaluated, as information on the research the author has undertaken for the work is, unlike with information books, seldom given. Nevertheless, considerable research is often necessary, for example for historical novels. Sometimes it is possible to find out what research the author has done because, although nothing may be mentioned in the book itself, the author describes his research methods and sources in an article he writes or in an interview he gives.

Observation In works of fiction the quality of the author's observation of human life, of the way people think, speak, and act, is often more significant than any background research he has undertaken. The strength of an author's observation can be seen in the detailed accuracy of it, which accuracy helps the reader to identify with and believe in the tale he is reading. Some authors keep notebooks of things they have seen and conversations they have heard, because they realize that these may yield invaluable raw material for their future stories.

Inventiveness Though some fiction is semi-autobiographical, it is the ability of the author to invent an imaginary story, characters and situations (sometimes a whole imaginary world) that singles out the masters of the fiction art. Admittedly, some types of fiction, for instance fantasy, probably call for more inventiveness than others, but all call for it to some extent. Inventiveness can be seen in the many ideas that some novels throw out and in the production of the clues that are given readers of detective stories, as well as in sheer imaginative ability.

Length The length of a fictional work, like that of an information book, is obviously affected by many considerations. It should be appropriate, for example, to the aim of the work, and should suit the theme and the plot. Sometimes critics of a novel state that its plot would be more suited to a short story. This is a reasonable condemnation of its length. Novels may also be condemned because they have been written to rule. That is, they have been concocted to fit a particular publisher's series whose titles are all of a standard length, probably about 75,000 words.

Plot This and the next two criteria deal with the basic ingredients of all fictional works, that is plot, setting and characters. The plot of a work may be outlined in the preliminary matter, if it is not stated on the dust jacket or cover. The relative importance of the plot will vary from book to book; for example, in a thriller it will tend to be more important, because action is necessary to thrillers, than in a novel that is chiefly concerned with the portrayal of character. The plot should be interesting, well worked out, and should have an overall cohesiveness and completeness. It cannot be expected that many plots will be particularly original; indeed the framework will often be a well-worn one, but the author of quality will find a way of giving new life to that framework.

Setting The time and the place chosen by the author in which to work out his plot are the setting of the book. The setting should be appropriate and believable. In some works, historical novels in particular, it needs also to be as accurate as possible. A successful setting provides the right kind of atmosphere for the story. There is virtually no limit to the settings that can be (and are) chosen by writers, and there is no doubt that an original kind of setting will tend to gain the attention and interest of the reader.

Characters There are essentially two kinds of characters, main characters and secondary ones. Both kinds should be shown as individual people and not just stereotypes. In many novels the characters need to be seen to develop as persons during the course of the story. In all fiction they should be seen to act in character throughout the story, as this will help the reader believe in them. Indeed, in some books the writer will be endeavouring to make the reader identify him or herself with the main character in it.

Level The choice of plot, setting and characters is obviously affected by the intellectual level of the work, which is in turn, clearly related to the book's aim and audience. Although level in fiction works, excluding children's publications, is of less importance than in information

96

books, it is certainly necessary to check that the level, as shown for example in the choice of characters, is suitable for the kind of reader for whom the book has been written.

Approach The author's approach includes how he selects his material. It also includes how he decides to put over his material, and when writing for children he must be careful not to write down to them. Detailed aspects of approach therefore include how much the author uses dialogue, and whether he writes in the first or third person. His approach includes too the decision as to how much to develop the story by revealing what is going on in the characters' minds as opposed to what they actually say and do. In addition, it includes deciding on the overall mood he wants to convey and the sort of vein in which he wants to write. The approach and the style of a work are therefore related criteria.

Style Style is an important criterion, and there are various aspects to it, for example, choice of words, mastery of grammar, use of figures of speech, and overall vitality. There are various questions relating to an author's style that the evaluator should ask. First, is the style consistent with the level of the book? Second, does the style have any particular strengths or weaknesses? An author may write good narrative passages, but be weaker on description, conversation or argument. Third, what sort of style does the writer possess? It may be basically simple but strong; on the other hand, it may be comparatively involved yet beautiful. As works of the imagination are to be savoured and enjoyed, a much more literary style than would be acceptable in an information book is often a positive advantage in them. A test of good poetry is that it sounds fine when read aloud. Good prose should also pass this test.

If the evaluator is examining fiction in translation, then it is difficult to tell how much the style is that of the original writer, and how much that of the translator. Of course, if he can read some of the book in the original, he will quickly solve this problem. The art of the translator, if successful, should result in a style that reflects the original, and that is also as easy to read. This is not easy to achieve whilst keeping the translation accurate.

Spirit The style and spirit of a book go together, in that the author's personality should be seen in both. The spirit of a work is deeper, though, being the stamp of the author's individual character. Spirit is more noticeable in literary than in popular fiction, as this is richer in thoughts and ideas, but it can be seen in some popular fiction when the writer's sincerity and integrity clearly come over.

The writer's attitudes also come over in many works of fiction, and they must be considered an aspect of the spirit of the book. It may be that the reader will not always be attracted by these attitudes, or indeed by the author's personality overall, but generally the reader (and the evaluator) prefers a book that is obviously the creation of a person who, like himself, has particular views and passions.

Permanence Compared with information books, works of fiction do not need to be updated; indeed, the charm of some novels now lies in the way they reflect the age in which they were written. However, the majority of fictional works have a limited life, in spite of not needing revision, simply because they do not contain sufficient spirit to survive for any length of time. For it is the spirit of a book which most makes it endure. As Milton memorably put it: 'A good book is the precious life-blood of a master spirit, embalmed and treasured up on purpose to a life beyond life'.[5]

Visual information Visual information in works of fiction usually consists of artists' drawings and paintings of various kinds. However, maps are also sometimes found, as are diagrams, for instance taking the form of a family tree. Far fewer adult novels are illustrated today than were a hundred years ago, although the more expensive issues of the classics are still illustrated together with most children's publications. The main value of illustrations in works of fiction, whether they are written for adults or children, is the same. It is not that they look attractive, it is that they add a further dimension to the story that is being told. In order to do this successfully, they need in fact to capture the full spirit of the text, as well as being of a high artistic standard. When they do capture it, as with Tenniel's illustrations to *Alice in Wonderland*, they become virtually inseparable from the text. Captions are not always added to illustrations accompanying fiction, and such illustrations are frequently not listed at the front of the work. These practices support the point made that the illustrations can almost be considered to be part of the text.

Supporting material This is rare in works of fiction, except for those editions of the classics which include both explanatory footnotes and editors' introductions. Such editions are often aimed at students, and certainly for students supporting material of any kind is invaluable.

Effect The evaluation of fiction is comparatively subjective, but this criterion is the most subjective of all. It is, however, very important, for a novel or short story which has no effect on the evaluator might just as well not have been written. Typically, good fiction moves the reader's emotions in some way, or at least leaves him with a feeling of satisfaction. It may also impress him intellectually. A great work of fiction will, in fact, communicate its spirit to the reader and have an effect on his spirit as well as on his mind and his emotions.

Power Fictional works belong to the literature of power,[6] and so the criterion of power needs to be included here. It is a criterion clearly related to the last one, as the more power the work contains, the greater is its likely effect on the reader. There are several kinds of power that the writer may possess, and some kinds are more important in certain types of fiction than in others. However, the first kind which needs to be considered by the evaluator is relevant to all fictional works and is especially important in those written for children. It is the power to hold the attention of the reader. The book which tells a story in such a manner that the reader accepts it as true has this kind of power, as does the book which has characters with whom the reader can readily identify. In fiction written for children, part of this power to command attention comes from the depth of the author's perception of the world of the child. The author's power to command attention should be obvious as soon as the book is begun to be read, as the opening of a book should immediately arouse the reader's interest.

The second kind of power is creative power, that is, the author's ability to create a world of his own. This kind of power is related to the power to hold the reader's attention, indeed the two kinds of power complement each other. Creative power is particularly of note in works of fantasy but is a feature of all kinds of novels.

The third kind of power found in fictional works is intellectual power. It is this kind of power that helps make the successful detective story. It is also relevant to those novels that argue a point of view as well as telling some sort of tale.

The fourth kind of power is the power to move the reader's emotions and stir his feelings. This power can be seen in many novels of a popular nature as well as in literary masterpieces.

Such masterpieces, however, alone contain a further kind of power, the power of insight. This is the power to reveal truths previously overlooked.

The last kind of power is also only found in the best fiction. It is a power that relates to the spirit of the book. If the personality of the author pervades the work in such a way that the reader deep down feels he is in communication with that personality, the work has spiritual power.

99

Children's fiction

Children's story books, which together with children's picture books make up children's or junior fiction, are available to suit all ages and abilities, and range from easy readers to teenage novels. Two of the criteria particularly relevant to them, Level and Visual information, have already been commented on earlier under children's information books. However, there are two other criteria that are also particularly relevant to story books, Effect and Approach.

Fictional works should obviously have an effect on child readers just as they have on adult ones, though it may be expected that they will extend the child's experience more than reading adult fiction will extend the adult's. Although the more ordinary story books may not offer much in the way of broadening horizons and enlarging experience, the better ones certainly will, and may indeed try to make the child more aware of the social and personal problems that he or she is likely to meet with in today's world. Those stories that deal with contemporary social and personal problems are especially likely to reveal through their authors' approach and attitudes particular viewpoints on matters such as race and sex.

There is current concern that, because of the considerable effect on children of what they read, all writers should take steps to see that in their stories, they promote, for example, racial attitudes which are appropriate for our multi-ethnic society. Of course, writers whose works were published in the past can be expected to reveal attitudes that were common when they were writing, but which are less common and acceptable today.

The evaluator, when dealing with recently published stories may reasonably expect their authors to encourage open-mindedness rather than prejudice in the child. To take the example of race again, a story dealing with our society may be expected to include characters from more than one race, and to show them as equals. It should also show its characters, no matter what race they are from, as individuals rather than as group stereotypes, and this approach should be reinforced by the book's illustrations. Ultimately, however, there can be no doubt that a standard approach by authors to problem issues such as race is undesirable. The author's approach must come out of the moral, religious, political and social values that he holds. Though it may be a good thing to protect a child for some time from the influence of certain kinds of authors, the day must come when he needs to be presented with and challenged by a variety of values and views.

100

Children's picture books Although most chidren's story books are illustrated, the tale they tell can be understood without pictures. This is not so with picture books, where the illustrations are an essential feature, and indeed some children's picture books consist entirely of illustrations. Picture books are, of course, the young child's introduction to reading, even though he is only likely to look at the pictures, the text being read to him, probably by his parents. But as well as introducing him to reading, picture books also aim to stimulate the child's imagination and to encourage him to make his own pictures. Picture books, although typically telling a story, can have more obviously educational uses, such as teaching the child his alphabet. They are a kind of book that in fact allow their creators to put over a surprisingly wide variety of content material, informational as well as fictional. They also allow it to be put over in a multitude of ways. The traditonal type of picture book has its illustrations supported by textmatter in the form of ordinary though large size type. But in many picture books today the textmatter is instead penned by the illustrator, sometimes with the words as in strip cartoons, that is, in balloon form.

It can be seen from the comments made about them, that the evaluation of picture books is a fairly specialized branch of evaluation. The main factors that need to be considered when their contents are examined are, however, fairly easily indicated.

The first is attractiveness. Picture books should be positively eye catching. The attractiveness of their contents cannot, of course, be separated from their design and production. Contents, design and production go together to create the appeal of a good picture book.

The second is how well the two parts of the contents, text and illustrations, harmonize. They should, in fact, be indivisible, balancing each other and revealing the same spirit. Overall they should be so integrated that the reader is left in no doubt that he is reading a picture book, not a book with pictures.

The third factor also concerns both parts of the contents. The story told by them should progress in such a way that each page links with the next.

The fourth factor concerns only the illustrations. They should be of a reasonable artistic standard, and should mix action, detail and atmosphere in the right proportions. As regards the detail, its particular value is that it invites the child to explore the pictures further.

The last factor just concerns the text. Because picture books contain few words, it is essential that each one counts.

If the evaluator considers these five factors, at the same time remembering the criteria that have been laid down in this and the previous chapter, then the assessment of picture books, though a comparatively specialized form of evaluation, should not prove difficult.

Other imaginative literature

The two main forms of imaginative literature, other than prose fiction, are poetry and plays. The criteria that have been applied to prose fiction can be applied to a large extent to these other forms, especially to plays, as plays have a plot, a setting and characters. Indeed, a full length play is in many ways like a novel, whilst a one act play is like a short story.

Plays Although the text of a play can be evaluated in much the same way as prose fiction, plays are seldom written to be read, they are written to be performed. This means that the evaluator, if he only reads them, can give but an incomplete judgement on them, indeed possibly an unfair judgement. Admittedly, the printed text of a play is accompanied by the playwright's stage directions, but the reading of these is hardly a substitute for seeing the play performed. The evaluator can take comfort, however, in the fact that few plays are printed until after they have proved a success on the stage.

The main points on which the evaluator judges the quality of a play are its plot, its characters, and its dialogue. The type of play will clearly determine the comparative importance of these three points. For instance, it is the action of the plot that is particularly important in a farce.

One problem the evaluator faces if he is selecting plays for a library collection is that many plays are published only in books of collected plays. This means, of course, that the evaluator often has to decide on the merit of a collection of plays rather than the purchasability of an individual drama. The library evaluator may also have the problem, if his library offers a service to local drama societies, of deciding what plays and collections of plays need to be provided, not just in the form of reading copies, but in the form of multiple copies for society use.

Poetry Poetry is obviously the hardest kind of imaginative literature to which to apply objective standards. Some criteria noted under prose fiction, Style, Spirit, Effect and Power in particular, are very relevant, but ultimately poetry defies any attempt to analyse it. Nevertheless there is no doubt that it is reasonable to apply certain tests to it, for
102

example, the test of being read aloud. The evaluator should also find that, unlike some prose fiction, poetry will repay rereading; indeed, it often needs rereading before it can be fully appreciated. The reason for this is that the poetic style of writing relies heavily on the ambiguity of its words. The meaning of a poem comes from what the writer implies as well as what he actually states. It is this style of writing that distinguishes poetry from prose almost as much as having rhythm and rhyme distinguish it. (The difference between poetry and verse, incidentally, may be considered to be that though verse shows skill in its composition, it lacks the poetic style as well as the poetic spirit.)

The evaluator's criteria when assessing poetry are, then, affected by its distinct nature, which also affects the method of examination that the evaluator adopts. Books of new poetry, unlike other new imaginative writings, do not normally need to be read right through. A modified skilful skim approach is quite sufficient. But after the evaluator has sampled a few of the poems and read them carefully, he should reread them before making up his mind about the book. Publications which are anthologies of previously published poems, as opposed to collections of new poems, can also be given a form of skilful skim, although if the evaluator is already familiar with many of the poems, an experienced glance at the anthology may suffice.

Notes and references

1 Broadus, R N *Selecting material for libraries* 2nd ed. New York, H W Wilson, 1981.

2 Thouless, R H *Straight and crooked thinking* London, Pan, 1974.

3 Subscription Books Committee *Manual* Chicago, American Library Association, 1969. The term subscription book is an American one for books that, because of their high cost, are sold on a hire-purchase basis.

4 When fictional works are considered, a separate criterion entitled 'Power' will be found to follow the one for 'Effect'.

5 Milton, J *Areopagitica* (1644).

6 As De Quincey put it: 'There is first the literature of knowledge and secondly, the literature of power'. De Quincey, T *Essay on the poets: Pope* (1848).

Chapter 6

PUBLISHED EVALUATIONS

Aids for the evaluator
This chapter is concerned both with surveying the types of publications which contain evaluations of books, and with commenting on those titles that are of most importance to the evaluator. It is, of course, the ninth state of the systematic method, *Obtaining second opinions*, that makes most use of published evaluations.

The evaluator not only needs to know about sources of published evaluations because he turns to them for opinions other than his own, but he can also learn from them something about how to evaluate books. Further, he will find them of value in that they will keep him up to date about what is happening in the book world, and especially about what is being published. The student evaluator should try to see as many sources of published evaluations as possible, and should not just look at them, but look at them critically, appraising both some of the individual assessments of books they contain, and also their overall contents.

There are so many sources of published evaluations that it would be impossible to cover them all. In fact, because the sources of published evaluations are constantly changing, a work that tried to give details of all of them would be out of date by the time it was published.

As well as published evaluations, information on books is available to the evaluator from two other forms of sources. These sources are not evaluative but are nevertheless of some use, especially in connection with book selection. The first gives nothing more than bibliographical details. The *British national bibliography* and Whitaker's *Books of the month and books to come* are examples of publications giving just this kind of information. Such publications are often called checklists; their main value lies in their covering many more titles than other forms of sources. Mere bibliographical details sometimes tell a book selector enough about a work to enable him to order

104

it, but they are clearly of no help when an assessment is required.

It should be noted that checklist information is becoming increasingly available from computer data bases such as BLAISE (British Library Automated Information Service) and that the information on these data bases can be retrieved in such a way as to suit the individual requirements of librarians and readers.

The second form that non-evaluative information about books takes is descriptive, that is, the source adds a few facts about the book to the bibliographical details of it. The most common source of such descriptive information is publishers' publicity material[1] though this naturally may promote books rather than just describe them. However, it is clearly not evaluative. The advertisement pages of trade periodicals like *The bookseller* are a further source of similar material.[2] An interesting form of descriptive information on books (see figure 5) is that put out about individual titles in slip or card format.[3] Sources of descriptive information about books may be of considerable use to the evaluator as, though they are not critical, they can give facts that are otherwise not easily ascertained. However, they are clearly of limited value compared with evaluative sources.

The rest of this chapter looks at the various types of sources containing evaluative information, dividing them into two main groups. The first is that concerned with evaluating newly published works; the second, that concerned with selecting and assessing the best books of the past. Within each of the two main groups, a number of types of sources can be identified, and each of these will be separately introduced.

New books

Book reviews of various kinds make up virtually all the sources of evaluative information on new books. These reviews may be oral, as on the BBC radio programme *Kaleidoscope*, but the reviewing sources of most use, and certainly those used most by librarians, are published ones. However, librarians do not use published book reviews in book selection as much as might be expected, though admittedly they use them for current awareness purposes as well as book selection ones. Their limited use of them in book selection is due to a number of reasons. Many book reviews are not written with librarians in mind, whilst many of the most penetrating reviews are only published a considerable time after the book's publication date.[4] But undoubtedly the main reason why book reviews are not more used in the library world is because librarians are often able to see the books themselves, and their personal evaluation of them is sufficient to enable a judgement to be made on their purchase.

There are four types of reviewing publications that librarians use, though only the last type is aimed at them. They may also read the book reviews (at the moment rather limited and based on those in certain periodicals) available on the *Prestel* viewdata service.

Newspapers and general periodicals Most newspapers include a few book reviews and in Britain the four serious Dailies, *The times, The financial times, The guardian* and *The daily telegraph*, together with the three Sundays, the *Sunday times, The observer* and the *Sunday telegraph*, are the most useful sources. However, they only cover a limited number of books, even though they may have extra reviews in certain issues, for instance at Christmas time. The number of books reviewed by such periodicals as *The listener, The new statesman, The spectator* and the American *Saturday review* is also limited but, like those in newspapers, their reviews are read by a large number of people, including many library users, who, having read the reviews in the latest issue, come to the library to borrow the books reviewed.

The several periodicals already mentioned are of a serious nature, but some more popular general periodicals are also useful sources of reviews, particularly a number of the women's magazines like *Cosmopolitan* and *She*.

Book and literary periodicals These publications specialize in reviewing books, and so are a more important type to the evaluator than the first. Sometimes they are associated with newspapers as, for instance, is the *Times literary supplement* and the *New York times book review*. On the whole they are aimed at the general reader, but they tend to cater too for academics, especially those who are concerned with the study of literature. These periodicals generally include, as well as reviews of varying length, news about books, and articles about writers. They may also feature poems and short stories. There are probably more noteworthy book and literary world periodicals being published in Britain today than for a number of years. The main reason for this is that in 1978-9 the *Times literary supplement* was affected by an industrial dispute, and three new publications came out to fill the gap caused by its absence, the *London review of books*, (at first issued with the *New York review of books*), the *Literary review* and *Quarto*.

Amongst the book and literary periodicals are quite a number that are just concerned with children's books, for example *Growing point*,

Books for your children, and the recently started *Books for keeps*, the journal of the School Bookshop Association. Within the periodicals devoted to children's books are several that have specialist approaches. For instance, *Dragon's teeth* is devoted to racial attitudes in publications for children. There is also the *School book review*, which has more of a specialist coverage than a specialist approach, being principally concerned with textbooks.

However, although the number of book and literary periodicals published in Britain seems to be growing, there is still none that reasonably covers popular information books. For that reason, the *Good book guide*, a sort of mail order catalogue, is worthy of mention. This compilation, though not really a reviewing journal, does include some evaluative comments, and its coverage of all kinds of popular publications is considerable.

Subject periodicals Three main kinds of subject periodicals exist, scholarly, professional and popular. The scholarly periodical, such as the *American journal of science* or the *British journal of educational psychology*, usually contains many authoritative (and sometimes long) book reviews written by experts for experts. It is in academic and special libraries that such periodicals are most likely to be used in book selection, and the student evaluator will find the reviews in them excellent sources to turn to for second opinions.

The reviews in professional periodicals like the *Solicitors' journal* and *Management today* are also most used in academic and special libraries. The reviews in these periodicals are, on the whole, similar to, if shorter than, those in the scholarly ones. Indeed, though some types of professional periodicals, such as trade journals, are basically practical, many approach their subjects in a fairly learned way.

The professional press in the field of education includes those periodicals aimed at teachers. The reviews in these frequently, as in the *Times educational supplement*, do not limit themselves to books on education, but cover also school textbooks and other publications for children. They are, therefore, of considerable importance to many librarians, especially school librarians, and not just to teachers.

Some popular subject periodicals, like the *Economist, New scientist* and *New society*, are rather like those general periodicals of a serious nature, being aimed at a similar audience, and having book reviews of similar titles as well as ones concerning their own subject fields. But most popular periodicals limit themselves to reviewing publications on the special interest of the magazine, as does the weekly periodical

Stamp collecting. The reviews in these popular subject periodicals may be less authoritative and, therefore, less valuable to the student evaluator than those in scholarly and professional subject journals, but they may be the only source for him of an evaluation of a particular title, especially if it is a popular information book.

Library world sources These may be divided into two main groups. The first comprises those professional journals that include not only reviews of books on librarianship, but reviews of books on other subjects in order to help librarians with their book selection. The second is made up of those periodicals that are produced basically as book selection aids. Both groups are of particular value to the student evaluator as well as to professional librarians because their reviews, though usually short, are aimed at the library world. There are only a few British library world sources published, but there are many such sources published in the United States, and these are in the main available in this country.

The best British example of the first group is the *School librarian*, which, however, is essentially limited to reviews of children's books. Apart from the *School librarian*, only one other British librarianship journal includes reviews for library book selectors, the *Library review*. Of the several American library periodicals that include a considerable number of reviews, the two outstanding titles are the *Library journal*, and the *School library journal*.

Turning to the second group, book selection periodicals, there is both an outstanding American and an outstanding British title: the American one is the *Booklist*, the British one, *British book news*. From both sides of the Atlantic there are also other important but slightly more specialized works, for example, *Choice*, a publication aimed mainly at American college librarians, and the *Aslib book list*, a tool aimed primarily at British special librarians.

There are, in addition, book selection periodicals, both American and British, aimed at children's librarians. Published in the United States is the *Horn book*; in Britain *Junior bookshelf*. These two periodicals, though mostly made up of reviews, do include some other bibliographical and literary features. There are also some publications of value to children's librarians put out by individual libraries, such as Hertfordshire County's *Material matters*.

Important reviewing journals
This section gives details of important or representative sources of reviews (many of the titles dealt with have already been mentioned).

A number are American publications which, although may only cover British books that have also been published in the United States, are relevant in that libraries in this country frequently buy American works. The titles are arranged by the kind of books they review and this not only complements the one given, but it roughly corresponds with the breakdown of the contents of books in the last chapter. First discussed are general sources, that is, sources that review all kinds of book; second, reviewing sources for information books (including, of course, quick-reference books); third, those for fiction; fourth, those for children's works both fiction and information books.

The student evaluator should obtain and examine as many as possible of the titles in this section, so as to learn more about them and appreciate their particular uses.[5] A few comments are therefore called for on what points should be looked for when reviewing sources are being appraised. These points are relevant to all reviewing sources, not just the ones dealt with below. Looking for these points will enable the evaluator to understand better the nature of the sources as well as enable him to judge their quality.

There are five points that should be looked for, and they may best be looked for in the following order. First, basic bibliographical information, such as the name of the publisher and the frequency of publication, should be sought. Second, the aim of the reviewing source and the audience for which its reviews are designed should be ascertained. These may not be stated in so many words, unless the source has a helpful sub-title, but the circulation figure may be given, however, and this will aid the evaluator to gauge the popularity of the publication. If it is not given within the publication itself, it may be obtained from such a work as *Ulrich's international periodical directory*.[6] Third, the overall contents of the reviewing source should be examined, the evaluator looking especially to see what kind of reviews are published, how many, and of what kind of books. He should at the same time note what other features, for example, articles, the source contains, and whether it has any special issues or supplements. He should also try to assess the up-to-dateness of the reviews by taking some sample titles, noting the date of the issue in which they were reviewed, and then comparing this with their publication dates. These will be most easily found from book trade publications such as Whitaker's *Books of the month and books to come*. Fourth, the evaluator should look to see if the names of the reviewers are given, and also their academic or professional posts. Lastly, the evaluator should assess how easy the reviewing source is to use. It should be clearly laid out, as well as systematically organized, and should have a detailed contents page and preferably an index with each issue in addition to annual or similar indexes.

General A number of important American sources are included under this heading, some because there is no British equivalent of them. Many general sources, for example, *Book choice*, have separate sections of reviews of paperbacks, but there is no reviewing source concerned exclusively with them.

1 *Books and bookmen* London, Brevet Publications, 1955-80, 1981- , monthly. After ceasing publication in 1980, another publisher began to issue this periodical in late 1981. Of general appeal, it is quite attractively produced. In its latest version annotated lists of books are featured as well as reviews. Similar but slightly more popular in its approach is *Book choice* (1981- , monthly), which came into being because of the suspension of *Books and bookmen*. *Book choice* has included an interesting series of interviews with editors of other reviewing sources entitled 'The book choosers'.

2 *Booklist* Chicago, American Library Association, 1905- , semi-monthly. This is a good aid for the student evaluator to study as it makes its reviewing policies and procedures clearer than most: a review in it is itself a recommentation. It has many wide ranging mini-reviews, including some of audio-visual materials, and it also has longer reviews of reference books in its 'Reference and subscription book reviews' section (once a separate publication). It is aimed mainly at American public and school librarians and is well used by them.

3 *British book news* London, British Council, 1940- , monthly. The outstanding British book selection tool for new books, it is particularly designed with overseas librarians in mind. It has about 3,000 mini-reviews a year, which are most often written by university or college teachers. Other regular features include a survey-review of older titles on a particular topic, a list of forthcoming publications and book world news items. From 1980 children's books are only covered three times a year in special supplements (excluding school textbooks). It arranges its reviews in a classified order and though they are sometimes little more than critical annotations, they cover the books on all subjects that librarians would generally class as basic works.

110

4 *Choice* Chicago, American Library Association, Association of College and Research Libraries, 1964- , monthly. The reviewing source most used by American college librarians, it has a very large number of mini-reviews, over 6,000 a year, and also has survey-reviews. A classified cumulation of the 60,000 books reviewed during its first ten years is available. As might be expected, it is a source for academic publications, not popular ones.

5 *Good book guide* London, Braithwaite and Taylor, 1977- , three issues a year. This is an interesting and attractive publication that is produced in connection with a mail-order bookselling service. Its reviews are really only critical annotations, but it covers many popular information works other sources overlook, and it sometimes features short comparative analyses of types of reference books.

6 *Library journal* New York, Bowker, 1876- , semi-monthly. The book review section of this professional journal is considerable, and there are regular special reviewing features in many of its issues. It is popular with public librarians in the United States, and its mini-reviews cover all kinds of books except children's works which are dealt with in the *School library journal* (at one time part of it). An annual cumulation of the reviews is available entitled *Library journal book review*.

7 *Publisher's weekly* New York, Bowker, 1872- , weekly. This book trade journal carries mini-reviews in its 'PW Forecasts' section. Although they are not very critical, they are considerably used by American librarians because they appear prior to the book's publication day. The equivalent British journal, *The bookseller*, does not at the moment carry similar regular reviews, though it does have occasional features covering books on particular topics which have the same kind of information. It also reviews recent reviews in 'Critics Crowner'.

8 *Times literary supplement* London, Times Newspapers Ltd, 1902- , weekly. Containing fairly detailed scholarly reviews of academic and other serious publications, this periodical has a high reputation. Its coverage, as its title implies, has a literary bias, and works on science and technology are virtually excluded. It deals with 50-75 titles in each issue, and has special issues with extra pages on certain subjects and types of books. As well as being indexed in *The times index*, its reviews can also be traced through its own annual index and its cumulative index volumes for 1902-1939 and 1940-1980. Apart from scanning its main contents, librarians can also scan its advertisement pages as they are a standard source of job vacancies in the library world. The *London review of books* and *The literary review* are com-

parable British reviewing sources, though they are really still establishing their place in the reviewing scene. The *Times educational supplement* and *Times higher education supplement* are not reviewing journals, but each includes several pages of appropriate reviews.

Information books It is more specialized information books that the general sources of reviews tend to overlook, and reviews of these are best sought in the subject journals covering the field of study required. However, there is also one noteworthy book selection aid for specialized information books: *Aslib book list* London, Aslib, 1936- , monthly. It originally covered just scientific and technical books, and basically is still only useful for these subject fields. The reviews, which are really critical annotations, are arranged by the Universal Decimal classification. Entries are given a symbol indicating the level of the book. This source is aimed at special librarians. Its American equivalent is the New York Public Library's *New technical books*.

Fiction Librarians often use the reviews in newspapers and general periodicals when seeking assessments of fiction, though the more literary fiction is, of course, covered by sources such as the *Times literary supplement*. For more popular fiction, women's magazines like *Cosmopolitan* are of more use. There is no reviewing source completely devoted to fiction.

Children's books As well as the many sources specializing in reviewing children's books (such as those below), a reasonable number of children's books are dealt with by 'General' sources. The so-called supplements to the *Times literary supplement* which are devoted to children's publications are especially of note.

1 *Growing point* Northampton, Margery Fisher, 1962- , bimonthly. It is basically the work of one person, yet is a highly acceptable publication. Its title page calls it: 'Margery Fisher's regular review of books for the growing families of the English reading world, and for parents, teachers, librarians and other guardians'. It includes a mixture of omnibus and mini-reviews, some of the latter being unusual in that they relate to older books, which are featured under the heading 'Reminders'.

2 *Horn book* Boston, Horn book, 1924- , bimonthly. This well-established American source has gained a high reputation over the years. In the United States it is probably the most used of the reviewing sources that specialize in children's books. There are 75-100 fairly short reviews in each issue, with emphasis being on fiction. Articles on children's literature are also a feature of its pages.

112

3 *Junior bookshelf* Huddersfield, Woodfield and Stanley, 1936- , bimonthly. This may be considered the British equivalent of the *Horn book* though it has fewer articles. Sub-titled 'A review of children's books', it is aimed at librarians and teachers. The reviews are short yet helpful: however, they sometimes take time to appear. This periodical has a high reputation and is the outstanding British book selection periodical for children's books.

4 *Material matters* Hertford, Hertfordshire Library Service, 1976- , bimonthly. This is an example of a tool produced by a particular library which has been found of use by other librarians. The reviews are no more than critical annotations, but are helpful nevertheless. Titles covered include some reprints. The reviewers are teachers, educational advisers, and librarians, and the periodical is produced by the Children's Book Assessment Panel of the library.

5 *School librarian* Oxford, School Library Association, 1937- , quarterly. The book reviews take up a considerable portion of the pages of this professional journal. Though short, the reviews are of a high standard and cover all age groups. Cumulative indexes of the reviews are available: *Index to fiction reviewed, 1970-79*; and *Recent information books: an index, 1976-80*.

Locating reviews

The evaluator needs to be able to locate book reviews of particular titles, even ones for books published many years ago, though it is not always easy to trace where and when a particular title received a review. The various methods and sources that may be used to locate individual reviews are, therefore, now outlined.

Cumulation of reviews in a particular publication It is unusual for a periodical to bring together all its reviews in an annual or other cumulation. However, the *Library journal* cumulates its reviews annually in the *Library journal book review*, whilst a multi-volumed cumulation of reviews from *Choice* is available as are ones from the 'Reference and Subscription Books Bulletin' part of the *Booklist*. Probably the most ambitious publication of this kind is the one that brings together (with indexes) the reviews published in the *New York times* between 1896 and 1970, and there are plans for updating this project.

Indexes to individual publications Although some newspapers and periodicals are not indexed at all, many have annual indexes and these are valuable for tracing reviews, especially as the evaluator can assume that the review will probably have appeared in the same year as the

113

book was published. Especially useful is the monthly *Times index* as this covers not only reviews appearing in *The times*, but also those in the *Sunday times*, the *Times literary supplement*, the *Times educational supplement* and the *Times higher education supplement*. In addition, a few periodicals have cumulative indexes covering a period of years, as does the *Times literary supplement*.

Indexes to book reviews The most notable way of tracing book reviews is through using those bibliographical tools that specialize in indexing them. Unfortunately, there is no British publication of this kind. Indexes to book reviews occasionally (as with *Book review digest*: see figure 6) include extracts from reviews in addition to references to them. Indexes to book reviews take two main forms, those that are published as periodicals and so index recent reviews, and those that are published in book form and index reviews that have appeared over a longer period of time. The outstanding ones in periodical form are the German *Internationale Bibliographie der Rezensionen wissenschaftlicher Literatur* (International bibliography of book reviews of scholarly literature), and the American publications *Book review digest*, *Book review index* and *Current book review citations* (see figure 7). There are also published in periodical form a few indexes to book reviews that are more limited in their scope, for example, the quarterly *Reviewers' consensus*, another American publication, which is just concerned with children's books.

It is indexes to books in book form, however, that mostly limit themselves to books of a more specialist kind. They also tend to cite reviews published over a long period of time; for example, the first part of the *Science fiction book review index* (published in the United States by the Gale Research Co.) covers 1923-1973. Indexes in book form, being generally more specialized, tend to be used less than those published as periodicals.

There are a few indexes to book reviews, such as the *Canadian book review annual* and the *American index to book reviews in the humanities*, which are published at yearly intervals, and these may be considered a cross between the two main forms. In addition, there is one publication, the *Children's literature review* which is a cross between a book review index and the kind of literary reference work about authors mentioned in chapter 4. It deals with different authors in each of its volumes and the considerable information given about each author includes copious quotations from both reviews and literary criticism of his books.

114

An annotated listing of book review indexes of every kind appeared in 1968 entitled *A guide to book review citations.*[7]

Those indexes to book reviews in periodical form already named as outstanding should be examined by the student evaluator in order that he may become more familiar with them, and further information on these titles is given below.

1 *Book review digest* New York, H W Wilson, 1905- , monthly. This is used as a book selection tool as well as an index to book reviews because its extracts from reviews makes some evaluation of the titles it covers possible. The number of sources it draws its reviews from is limited, and it deals with no more than about 6,000 books a year. Titles are only included if at least two reviews (four for fiction) can be found for them. The quotations from reviews try to reflect the balance of reviewers' opinions. Cumulations are available, together with a *Book review digest: author/title index, 1905-1974.*

2 *Book review index* Detroit, Gale Research Co., 1965- , bimonthly. This is better than the *Book review digest* for more specialized books, though, of course, only bare citations are given. It aims to cover 80,000 reviews of 40,000 new books a year, and cumulations include *Book review index: a master cumulation*, 1969-1979. The *Children's book review index* is drawn from the main work.

3 *Current book review citations* New York, H W Wilson, 1976- , monthly. This is similar to *Book review index*, and indeed the coverage of the two publications overlaps to a great extent. The largest cumulations so far available are annual ones.

4 *Internationale Bibliographie der Rezensionen wissenschaflicher Literatur* Osnabruck, Dietrich, 1971- , fascicules. Often referred to by the abbreviation IBR, this international bibliography of book reviews of scholarly literature is by the publishers of the famous IBZ (*International bibliography of periodical literature*). It is a work with multilingual features, and its main arrangement is by subject. Bound volumes of it are also available.

Indexes to periodical articles These indexes will usually only be turned to when using indexes specifically for book reviews has failed to turn up any references. The reason why indexes to periodical articles may be of use to the evaluator is that some not only index the articles in the periodicals they cover, they also index the book reviews which appear in these periodicals. For instance, most of the indexes put out by the American firm of H W Wilson (such as the *Readers' guide to periodical literature*) carry a separate sequence of references to book reviews. The citation form of index[8] may also be found of use in tracing book reviews.

Periodicals with a review of reviews feature This occasionally found feature is not so much an index to reviews as a collection of extracts from them. For the subject area of librarianship the *Journal of academic libraianship* in its 'JAL guide to new books and book reviews' will be found (to a limited extent) to review reviews. Also aimed, at least in part, at librarians is the 'Indexes reviewed' feature of the journal *The indexer.* This extracts comments from published reviews of books on all subjects, but limits itself to extracting the reviewers remarks about the publication's index. It is therefore unusual in its approach, which is interesting also for its arrangement. The feature is divided into 'Indexes praised', 'Indexes censored', and 'Indexes omitted'.

Book-guides with references to reviews Sometimes guides to good books (still to be dealt with in this chapter) not only have entries with critical annotations, but include in these annotations references to, and perhaps quotations from, published book reviews. Such references and quotations are now, for example, a feature of the two most important guides to the best reference books, the Library Association's *Guide to reference material* (see figure 8), and the American Library Association's *Guide to reference books.*

Best books
Those bibliographies and book lists, published as books, pamphlets, or as periodical articles, that indicate the best books on a subject or those that a certain kind of library should buy, are important to librarians because of the help they give in the selection of older material. (However, some of them deal with fairly recent works, selecting their material from the publications of the year just finished.) But in spite of their value, librarians do not use them as much as might be expected. This is possibly because the books recommended in them may not be available for purchase, being out of print. Librarians prefer to select older material from the shelves of library suppliers as this method of selection means they are choosing from stock which is currently available, as well as having the advantage of letting them see the books themselves. They also may select from library suppliers' catalogues, which although only usually lists of books, consist of titles that are both available and that have proved popular in libraries over the years.

Guides to good books are less valuable to the evaluator than book reviews as the critical comments they contain are much shorter, but
116

they are still useful sources from which to obtain a second opinion. Some guides to best books are compiled for librarians, but others, although used by librarians are compiled for readers.

Although book-guides are the main source of evaluative information concerning best books, several other kinds of sources may also be found of use, and these are dealt with later. Book-guides themselves may be divided into four types according to the kind and amount of guidance they give.

Unannotated lists This is the type of guide which gives least information about its titles. Indeed, it usually gives only basic bibliographical information for each of its entries, although it may include further information in the form of symbols, for example, an asterisk may mean strongly recommended. But, although this kind of book-guide lacks annotations, the fact that a work has been selected for inclusion is generally a recommendation in itself. However, a few guides indicate that their books are no more than a representative collection of titles. This is true, for example, with those put out in the series, *The 'Librarian' subject guide to books* and with Bruce Stevenson's *Reader's guide to Great Britain.*

Annotated lists This type is an important one, and there are several very valuable titles and series that belong to it. The annotations in this type of book-guide, as was mentioned when the compilation of book-guides was discussed in chapter 3, vary in nature as well as in length. They may be just descriptive, but they may be critical, and even (as noted in the last section) include references to and quotations from reviews. The annotated book-guide, then, can be of considerable aid to the evaluator.

Four organizations that produce a number of annotated lists, some in the form of a series and most of pamphlet size, are the National Book League, the Library Association's Youth Libraries Group, its Public Libraries Group, and the School Library Association. An example of the publications of the last named organization is *Fiction, verse and legend: an annotated guide to the selection of imaginative literature for middle and secondary schools*, edited by D Warren. Like the School Library Association's guides, those published by the Youth Libraries Group of the Library Association are aimed at teachers as well as librarians. An example from their pamphlet series of guides is *Multi-racial books for the classroom.* The pamphlet series put out by the Public Libraries Group, on the other hand, is aimed at the general reader. The guides in this series, such as those on *British archaeology*

117

and *Wales*, however, are sometimes used by librarians to help them revise their stock. The National Book League issues book-guides designed for a wide range of users, but parents and teachers are especially well catered for, for example, in the annual selection of best children's books, *Children's books of the year*. Many of the National Book League's guides, like this one, are produced for use with an appropriate book exhibition.

It is guides from the annotated list group that make up the majority of the titles selected for further comment. Additional examples to those above will be found, therefore, amongst these titles.

Survey-reviews Survey-reviews, as defined in chapter 3, are articles that select and survey with brief comments a considerable number of books on a particular subject. As such surveys are seldom of new books, these reviews are more appropriately included in this section than with other reviewing sources. The main value of survey-reviews is probably their coverage of subjects too specialized to merit a guide in book or pamphlet form. They are also of value because, being written in narrative fashion, they enable the writer to bring complementary titles together and relate them to each other. The writer's comments on each title are commonly very short, and so survey-reviews are of limited value to the evaluator.

The outstanding example of a British book periodical with a regular survey-review is *British book news*; the best American example is probably *Choice*. This has also featured a variation on the survey-review theme — the May 1981 issue surveys its selection of 'Outstanding academic books, 1980' just by listing them, but gives a reference against every entry to when the work was reviewed in its pages.

Comparative analyses These are detailed comments on publications, the books being either directly compared (ie the best buy or *Which?* report approach), or the information about each title is set out in a standard manner, allowing for easy comparison. Because of their detailed treatment of titles, comparative analyses are clearly of considerable use to the evaluator. They may also be of interest to him because they may analyse all the titles within a particular type of book rather than just a selection of them.

The Consumers' Association, publishers of *Which?*, have in fact carried out at least one comparative analysis, children's encyclopaedias in January 1964. The *Which?* kind of report is not aimed at librarians, though obviously it is of value to them: it is aimed at consumers, like ordinary book buyers. However, there are some similar analyses

118

aimed at librarians. There is, for example, a regular feature in the American periodical *Reference services review* entitled 'Comparative review', which aims to aid the purchase of reference tools by pointing out the similarities and differences between titles within a group of similar publications. Another American publication is a good example of the kind of analysis which results in information and comments about books being set out in a standard way. It is Kenneth Kister's *Dictionary buying guide* which aims to help anybody wanting to buy a dictionary. This second kind of comparative analysis can easily cover a large number of titles, as does Kister, and may, therefore, like his work, be of book length. The *Which?* report kind of analysis is much shorter and is limited to a small number of titles.

As can be seen from the examples above, the analysis form of book-guide seems to have been mainly produced for reference books, probably because they are expensive to buy, and because they lend themselves to a comparative approach.

Important guides to best books

This section gives information about important guides to best books, arranged as was the section dealing with important sources of reviews. The student-evaluator should try to examine as many of the book-guides introduced here as possible since he will in that way learn more about their nature and variety as well as learning better how to use them. When guides to best books are being examined, six particular points should be looked for, and the guides assessed against these points.

First, basic bibliographical details, such as the publisher's name, the date of publication, and the existence of previous editions, should be ascertained. At the same time, the publication of any related works should be noted. Second, the aim and the audience of the guide should be discovered; it is most likely to be stated in its introduction. Third, the scope of the contents must be considered. Amongst the questions that the evaluator should ask is: are all the books recommended in print? Fourth, the selection of the contents should be examined. Is it made clear who has been responsible for their selection?; are the criteria on which the selection has been based given? The fifth point for the evaluator to look for is the amount of information provided on each title included. Is it limited to the bibliographical details of the book; or are notes, annotations, and possibly symbols added? Lastly, the arrangement, indexing, and ease of use of the guide needs to be assessed.

Especially to be looked for is whether author, title, and subject approaches are all catered for.

General There is, unfortunately, only one British book-guide worthy of a main entry under this heading. Two American publications also merit inclusion, but the evaluator should note that they, and the other United States guides given under subsequent headings, naturally have a different emphasis as regards their contents than have British ones.

1 Prakken, S L, ed. *The reader's adviser: a layman's guide to literature* 12th ed, New York, Bowker, 1974-8, 3v. At one time known as the *Bookman's manual*, this is a large-scale work which aims to cover the best books in print. The emphasis is literary. Authors are given introductory paragraphs, but annotations to individual books are generally short, although some quotations from reviews are to be found. There is no British equivalent to this work.

2 Raphael, F and McLeish, K *The list of books* London, Mitchell Beazley, 1981. This annotated reading list is divided into a variety of headings and covers over 3,000 titles. Many symbols are used to aid its evaluations. It is hoped the work will be revised every two years. Another recent publication of the same kind is Philip Ward's *A lifetime's reading* (Cambridge, Oleander, 1981).

3 Weber, J S, ed. *Good reading: a guide for serious readers* 21st ed, New York, Bowker, 1978. Subject chapters by specialist contributors take up the most part. Each subject (or literary form) is briefly introduced, and there then follows a critically annotated booklist. This guide's approach is worth comparing with the more popular and superficial approach of the British work, *The list of books.*

Information books – predominantly reference works

1 Sheehy, E P, ed. *Guide to reference books* 9th ed, Chicago, American Library Association, 1976. The American equivalent to Walford, it may still be found referred to as Winchell, the name of its most famous compiler. The two works complement each other to some extent, in that this one has more North American titles. There are good annotations, with some references to reviews. A supplement was published in 1980.

2 Walford, A J, ed. *Guide to reference material* 4th ed, London, Library Association, v.1- , 1979- . The 'Bible' for British reference librarians, a guide that is now also available in a single volumed version, *Walford's concise guide to reference material.* The full work is now in three volumes (issued a subject volume at a time), the last complete

120

edition being the third (1974-7). Coverage is considerable. It has over 12,000 entries, and they are reasonably international. The annotations are sometimes critical, and there are occasional references to and quotations from reviews.

3 Wilson, H W, Co. *Public library catalog* 7th ed, New York, Wilson, 1978. Four annual supplements (1979-82) are planned to update this American book selection tool covering non-fiction books. This updating plan, and indeed the other basic features of this work, are to be found in most of this publisher's series of related book-guides. The selection of titles is by librarians and the annotated entries, which are in Dewey order, include quotations from reviews. The work is most used by United States public libraries.

4 Wynar, B S, ed. *American reference books annual* Littleton, Libraries Unlimited, v.1- , 1970. This is an unusual publication as it aims to review all reference books, as opposed to a selection of them. It is unusual, too, in that it contains mini-reviews rather than just annotations. At the end of these reviews references to other reviews are sometimes given. A selection from the first seven years of this work was issued in 1976, *Best reference books, 1970-76*. There is now another American annual on reference books, *Reference sources* (Ann Arbor, Pierian Press, 1977-), which should be compared with this one. It will be found that *Reference sources* is a cross between a book-guide and an index to book reviews.

Fiction For both fiction and other imaginative literature, the reference works on authors cited in chapter 4 may also be referred to, together with M Seymour-Smith's *Novels and novelists* (London, Windward, 1980).

1 Baker, E A and Packman, J *A guide to the best fiction* 3rd ed. London, Routledge, 1932 (reprinted 1967). This British work covers about 10,000 titles including ones translated into English. Its annotations are sometimes quite lengthy. A supplement covering 1931-60 is in active preparation.

2 Wilson, H W, Co. *Fiction catalog* 10th ed, New York, Wilson, 1980. Aimed mainly at American public librarians, this is a well-accepted guide to adult fiction. Its annotations incorporate quotations from reviews, and its arrangement incorporates a subject approach. Four annual supplements (1981-4) will keep it up to date.

Children's books – fiction and information books

1 Mortimer, S M *What shall I read? a select list of quality books for children* 2nd ed, London, Library Association, 1978. This is prob-

ably the best British annotated list of good children's works, though there are others. An American publication worth comparing with it is *The best in children's books* by Zena Sutherland (University of Chicago Press, 1974), which is based on reviews appearing in the University's valuable reviewing periodical, *Bulletin of the center for children's books*.

2 National Book League *Children's books of the year* London, National Book League in conjunction with Julia MacRae Books, 1971- , annual. Each year this exhibition catalogue covers a selection of about 300 of the best children's books, and has established a high reputation as a reliable book-guide because of its perceptive critical annotations. Compiled originally by Elaine Moss, it is now the work of Barbara Sherrard-Smith.

3 Wilson, H W, Co. *Children's catalog* 14th ed, New York, Wilson, 1981. This is the basic American guide to works for younger children, while the publisher's *Junior High School library catalog* (4th ed, 1980) and *Senior High School library catalog* (11th ed, 1977) cover those for older children. All three works have four annual supplements. Annotated entries with use of quotations from reviews are a feature of the three works.

Locating book-guides

Most book-guides, as they are in the form of separately published books or pamphlets, are more easily traced than are book reviews. They are listed in well-known bibliographies like the *British national bibliography*, whilst those stocked by a particular library will also have entries in the library's catalogue. However, the evaluator will find it helpful to have a few comments on the methods and sources most relevant to the location of book-guides. Some of these sources, incidentally, also include information about book reviewing periodicals. There is no need to single out individual sources for further comment as was done with important book review indexes, but those sources which annotate rather than just list are, of course, usually the most valuable. Sources for tracing book-guides may be divided into three main groups.

Guides to book selection tools Few guides of this kind exist as separate publications. However, there may be relevant chapters in guides to best books such as the American Library Association's *Reference books for small and medium sized libraries*, where chapter 1 is devoted to 'Selection aids for reference materials'. Of the separately published guides to book selection tools, three may be noted. The most general is the British Council compilation (see figure 9), *Aids in the selection of British books*,[10] which, if it were revised and extended, would be an invaluable tool. The other two relate to children's books, a leaflet published in Britain entitled just *Guides to book selection*,[11] and the larger American publication whose full title is *Selecting materials for children and young adults: a bibliography of bibliographies and review sources.*[12]

Besides guides to book selection tools there are three other kinds of bibliographies which the evaluator may find especially useful. They are bibliographies of bibliographies, guides to reference books and literature guides. Also commented on are those textbooks in librarianship which include information on book-guides.

Bibliographies of bibliographies The *Bibliographic index*,[13] another of the publications of the H W Wilson Company, lists with its bibliographies book-guides of various kinds, and indeed has amongst its sub-headings under 'Books and reading' one for 'Best books'. The *Bibliographic index* obviously emphasizes American compilations; on the other hand it has the advantage, as it comes out three times a year, of being up to date. While the *Bibliographic index* covers all subjects, most bibliographies of bibliographies are more specialized in their scope, for example, the School Library Association's *A guide to book lists and bibliographies for the use of schools.* Unlike some, this, like the *Bibliographic index*, includes entires for lists which are only part of a book or periodical.

Guides to reference books These publications, like Walford's *Guide to reference material*, will be found to include book-guides. As a rule they also have annotations, and this adds to their value. In Walford the main consideration of book-guides is in Volume 3 under the heading 'Reading' (Dewey number 028).

Literature guides These are bibliographical publications which contain textbook features, as they try to teach students, research workers and librarians about the important kinds of information sources which exist for particular subject fields. Some of them deal with book-guides better than others; an example of one which clearly has a chapter relevant to the evaluator is Rogers's *The humanities: a selective guide to information sources*, as chapter 2 of this work is entitled 'General reference and selection aids in the humanities'. Many literature guides are listed in the previously mentioned British Council's *Aids in the selection of British books.*

Librarianship textbooks Most textbooks on book selection (a

123

WUORINEN, Charles
Simple composition/by Charles Wuorinen. — Longman Inc. (dist. Longman UK),
21.1.80. — 192p.: musical examples; 26cm. — Longman music ser. —
ISBN 0-582-28059-1 Paperback: £7.95.

SCOPE: Survey of twentieth-century music composition which provides practical
details of compositional procedures & devices.

CONTENTS: The basic nature of the 12-tone system; On the 12-tone system: fundamental principles & definitions; The surface of compositions; Surface; Rhythm;
Melody; Revision; Structure; The 12-tone pitch system: elements & operations;
The 12-tone pitch system: further operations; The 12-tone pitch system: extensions; Rhythmic organisation: the time-point system; Form; Form & composition;
Formal organisation; extending the time-point system; Valedictory; Index; Bibliography.

READERSHIP: Second & third year undergraduates specialising in twentieth-
century music composition.

AUTHOR: Composer & winner of the Pullitzer Prize.

Figure 5   Systematic descriptive information about books

ROBERTS, G. C. K. ed. Drug action at the
molecular level; report of a symposium held on 12
and 13 April 1976 at Middlesex hospital medical
school, London. 1977
    Brit Bk News p 134 F '78. M. F. G. Stevens
ROBERTS, J. I. ed. Beyond intellectual sexism;
a new woman, a new reality. 1976
    Contemp Psychol 22:933-4 D '77. L. A. Peplau
ROBERTS, N. ed. Use of social sciences literature. 1977
    J Doc 33:169-70 Je '77. C. Harris
    Lib Q 48:90-2 Ja '78. D. Bergen
ROBERTS, T. B. ed. Four psychologies applied
to education. 1975
    Educ Res 20:257-8 F '78. A. Smithers
ROBERTS, W. B. Minden curse; il. by S. Streeter.
1978
    Bklist 74:1438 My 1 '78. B. Elleman
ROBERTSON, D. Sir Charles Eastlake and the
Victorian art world. 1978
    Lib J 103:1052 My 15 '78. W. J. Dane
ROBERTSON, E. G. and Robertson, J. Cast iron
decoration; a world survey. 1977
    Ind Design 24:21 N '77. J. R. Guilfoyle
ROBERTSON, J. C. Guide to radiation protection.
1977
    Sci Bk 13:214 Mr '78. W. G. Stanziale
ROBERTSON, W. Free to act; how to star in
your own life. 1978
    Lib J 103:1182 Je 1 '78. M. A. Pradt
ROBINSON, B. Sailor's tales. 1978
    Lib J 103:742 Ap 1 '78. D. C. Rowland
ROBINSON, D. N. Psychology; traditions and pre-
spectives. 1976
    Contemp Psychol 23:142-51 Mr '78. J. A.
Popplestone
ROBINSON, J. In extremity; a study of Gerald

ROHAN, P. and Reskin, M. Real estate transac-
tions: condemnation procedures & techniques—
forms, v 3-3B. 1977?
    Urban Law 10:168-71 Wint '78. D. R. Levin
ROHN, P. H. Treaty profiles. 1976
    Am J Int L 71:800-3 O '77. Z. J. Slouka
ROHN, P. H. World treaty index. 5v. 1974
    Am J Int L 71:800-3 O '77. Z. J. Slouka
ROLFE, B. Behind the mask. 1977
    Educ Theatre J 29:581-2 D '77. H. Huston
ROMIG, D. A. Justice for our children; an exam-
ination of juvenile deliquent rehabilitation pro-
grams. 1978
    Lib J 103:770 Ap 1 '78. V. P. Schmidt
RONZITTI, N. Le guerre di liberazione nazionale
e il diritto internazionale. 1974
    Am J Int L 71:826-7 O '77. F. Pocar
ROOTS, J. M. Chou; an informal biography of
China's legendary Chou En-lai. 1978
    Bklist 74:1238 Ap 1 '78
    Chr Sci Monitor p23 Ap 19 '78. R. Kilborn, jr
    Lib J 103:758 Ap 1 '78. S. I. Levine
ROPER, R. On Spider creek. 1978
    Lib J 103:1083+ My 15 '78. K. Bosch
RORVIK, D. M. In his image; the cloning of a
man. 1978
    Bk World pE1+ Ap 16 '78. R. Goodell
    Lib J 103:1049 My 15 '78. L. Bartolini
ROSA, A. F. and Eschholz, P. A. Contemporary
fiction in America and England, 1950-1970; a guide
to information sources. 1976
    Bklist 74:1380-1 Ap 15 '78
ROSAND, D. and Muraro, M. Titian and the Ven-
etian woodcut. 1976
    Art Bull 59:637-41 D '77. C. Karpinski
ROSE, A. Spider in the sky; il. by G. Owens. 1978
    Sch Lib J 24:76 Ap '78. A. S. Phy

Figure 6   Indexing of books reviews, entries from *Current
book review citations*

GUNSON, NIEL, ed. The Changing Pacific. See
The Changing Pacific.

GURDUS, LUBA KRUGMAN. The death train; a
personal account of a holocaust survivor. 166p il
$10 '78 National Council of Art in Jewish life;
for sale by Schocken bks.

940.53 Jews—Persecutions—Personal narratives.
World War, 1939-1945—Jews in Poland
ISBN 0-89604-005-4   LC 78-54657

"Gurdus, an artist, tells her story in both drawings and words. During the Nazi Occupation of
Poland, she loses her parents, her baby, and tem-
porarily, her husband. She manages to survive by
hiding with friends and, finally, by means of faked
Polish work papers. For nearly seven years she
flees from place to place.... In Zwierzyniec the
cattle trains roll by her house; in Chorbrzany a
gray mass of people moves along the road below
her; in Warsaw thousands fill the road into the
Ghetto; and when she gets to Maydanek [concen-
tration camp], the corpses are wheeled by in open
carts." (Library J)

"After the war [Gurdus] made a series of drawings—of ghettos and ghetto fighters, of escaping
children, of deportation marches and death trains
—some of which illustrate her remarkably re-
strained memoir." M. S. Cosgrave
            Horn Bk 55:460 Ag '79 140w

"Gurdus has reproduced her indelible impressions in the most shattering drawings I have ever
seen." Gerda Haas
            Library J 104:623 Mr 1 '79 140w

HADDON, CELIA. Be beautiful; the country way.
(Country Way Bk) 63p $4.95 '79 Summit Bks.

HANSER, RICHARD. A noble treason; the revolt
of the Munich students against Hitler. 319p pl
$12.50 '79 Putnam

943.086 Germany—History—1933-1945. World
War, 1939-1945—Underground movements
ISBN 0-399-12041-6   LC 78-20832

Hanser examines "the factors that prompted
Hans Scholl and his sister Sophie, leaders of the
small student anti-Nazi movement, into active
opposition. [He argues that] his subjects were
idealists, but not fools. Instead they misjudged
the strength of the system they challenged and
the capacity of their fellow Germans to pass by
on the other side." (Library J) Index.

———

"Richard Hanser employs a high-key journalis-
tic style to dramatize the history of this resistance group of little fame and less evident ac-
complishment. Readers seeking a well docu-
mented, unemotional account will cringe when
encountering unreferenced superlatives such as
this: 'As examples of moral heroism, the actions
of 'the White Rose' are unsurpassed in European
history or 'Hitler's own army was the seed
bed of the most damaging resistance against
him.' Nevertheless, Hanser's account does provide a realistic picture of the atmosphere of
paranoia and repression which so long dominated
life in Nazi Germany. This book should be added
to library collections which already own, or are
prepared to obtain, Inge Scholl's version of the
same story called Students Against Tyranny [BRD
1970]." Joseph Barth
            Best Sell 39:259 O '79 390w

"Studies of the German Resistance often present the men and women of the 'White Rose' as
quixotic idealists, important only for their early
public defiance of Hitler's regime. Hanser en-
larges this picture.... This is a compelling popular supplement to such scholarly histories as
Peter Hoffmann's The History of the German

Figure 7 Indexing and quoting of book reviews, entries from *Book review digest*

8 Literature

Bibliographies

8:016

MODERN LANGUAGE ASSOCIATION OF AMERICA. MLA international bibliography of books and articles on the modern languages and literatures. New York, M.L.A., 1922-. Annual. (1976 annual. 1977. 3v. in 1 (xxxv, 312p.; xxxvi, 386p.; xxvii, 204p.). (1978 ed. 1979. $75).

Title varies. As *American bibliography*, 1921-55.
The 1976 annual has 3 main parts: 1. General, English, American, Medieval and Neo-Latin, Celtic literature. Folklore — 2. General Romance, French, Italian, Spanish, Portuguese and Brazilian, Romanian, General Germanic, German, Netherlands, Scandinavian, Modern Greek, Oriental, African and East European literatures — 3. Linguistics (8,699 references). Each main part has an author index. Parts 1 and 2 total 32,283 references. No annotations, but a very thorough listing.
'While it falls short of comprehensiveness, it picks up virtually all major contributions to philological scholarship. Furthermore it covers many areas for which there is inadequate current bibliographical coverage (*eg*, neo-Latin literature)' (*Library trends*, v.15, no.3, January 1967, p.580).

8:016

The Reader's adviser: a layman's guide to literature. 12th ed., edited by Sarah L. Prakken. New York & London, Bowker, 1974-77. 3v. $69.95, the set; ea. $25; ea. £18.

First published 1921 as *Bookman's annual*. 11th ed., 1968-69 (2v.).
    v.1: *The best in American and British fiction, poetry, essays, literary biography, bibliography and reference*. 1974. xx, [1], 808p.
    2: *The best in American and British drama, and world literature in English translation*. 1977. xiii, [1], 774p.
    3: *The best in the reference literature of the world*. 1977. xiii, 1034p.
The *Guide* aims 'to include the best of the 365,000 volumes listed in *Books and print* for 1973-74'. V.1 has 16 chapters, each with an introductory essay. Helpful notes on authors ('W.M. Thackeray': 2p., giving a literary appreciation, listing editions and noting books about Thackeray). V.3, with its deceptive title, actually covers all literature that is not belles lettres (*eg*, 1. Reference books in general — 2. General biography and autobiography — 3. Bibles and related texts... 7. Science... 12. Travel and adventure).
A valuable selection aid for the layman, librarian and bookseller (although imprints are naturally US).

Manuals

8(021)

SEYMOUR-SMITH, M. Guide to modern world literature. London, Wolfe, 1973. xxi, 1206p. £10.

US ed. as *Funk & Wagnalls Guide to modern world literature* (1973; New York, Crowell. $17.50). The paperback ed. (Hodder & Stoughton, 1975. 4v. £8, the set) is specially revised and updated.
A series of 33 essays on national literatures or linguistic groups of literatures (African and Caribbean literature — Albanian literature — American literature (p.23-174)... Yugoslav literature). That on British literature occupies p.191-323. The scope extends to writers of all nationalities who had survived as at 31 December 1899, although it embraces such writers as Hopkins, Mallarmé, who died before that date. Includes quotations, all in English. Select bibliography of reference works and critical studies, p.1135-42; index (over 8,000 entries), p.1143-1206. Subjective; welcomed for readability and erudition. 'Unlike the compilers of most reference tomes, Mr. Seymour-Smith has strong views about the authors he includes and does not hesitate to utter them' (*The Financial Times*, 25 October 1975, p.33).

Encyclopaedias & Dictionaries

8(031)

BENÉT, W.R., ed. The reader's encyclopedia. 2nd ed. New York, Crowell; London, Black, 1965. viii, [1], 1118p. £6.50. (Revised reprint, 1966. 2v. $15.95).

First published 1948; suppt..1955.
About 25,000 entries, — biographies, synopses of important works, characters in novels and plays, myths, legends and folklore. The 2nd ed. omits some material in the 1st ed. but contains 19% more text and pays more attention to the literatures of the Near and Far East, the USSR and Latin America. 'A guide to pronunciation of foreign or the most difficult names would have been a boon' (*Library journal*, v.90, no.2, 15 January 1965), p.229-30).
E.C. Brewer's *The reader's handbook of famous names in fiction, allusions, references, proverbs, plots, stories and poems* (New ed. London, Chatto, 1898. viii, 1501p. Reprinted Detroit, Mich., Gale, 1966. 3v. $29.50), first published 1879) is valued for its ample coverage. Synopses of plots under titles of works. Complementary to *Brewer's Dictionary of phrase and fable* (qv).

Figure 8   Quotations from book reviews in a book-guide, *Walford's Concise guide to reference material*

31b THE BOOKSELLER, Spring and Autumn Numbers, 90p per copy if bought separately; included in the annual subscription.

Lengthy blurb articles of books published in the previous half-year are classified under some 27 subjects (such as fiction, poetry, natural history, reprints and paperbacks) and there are publishers' lists, statistics of output during that half-year, and an index to books advertised, etc.

32 BOOKS OF THE MONTH AND BOOKS TO COME, Whitaker, 60p per copy, £7.20 p.a.

Contains a list of the past month's books taken from the *Bookseller* and those due to be published during the next two (the latter marked with an asterisk). It generally comes out about 3 weeks after the cumulated month ends.

c Reviewing Journals

Reviews in scientific journals are a particularly important aid in book selection (see Sections III and VII below).

For literature and the arts, no one can decide whether reviews really boost sales, but whether they are good or bad, they certainly stimulate interest among British readers and bookbuyers and are widely read and quoted. They have the sort of prestige in this country that literary prizes, little regarded here, have on the Continent of Europe. The major dailies, *The Times, Guardian, Daily Telegraph, Financial Times,* and *Evening Standard* all carry regular book pages. The Sunday papers, the *Observer, Sunday Telegraph,* and *Sunday Times* have complete sections on the preceding week's arts, including book pages, with reviews by leading writers. Prestigious weeklies such as the *New Statesman, Spectator, Economist, Listener* and *Punch* are another source of serious book reviews. Although the *Times Educational Supplement* has reviews of educational books, only the *TLS* (no. **34**) is entirely a book journal. Journals and proceedings of learned societies often carry scholarly reviews of books in their field.

33 BRITISH BOOK NEWS, British Council, monthly, 20p per copy, £2.40 p.a. in the UK.

Some 230 books are reviewed monthly, classified by Dewey and with fuller bibliographical detail than is usual in most reviewing journals. There is also a bibliographical article and news from publishers, and a list of forthcoming titles on an 8-page insert. An index is given annually. The nearest equivalent to the American book selection journal, *Choice.*

34 TIMES LITERARY SUPPLEMENT (TLS), weekly, published on Thursday, 12p per copy, £8.32 p.a.

A very long article on an important book precedes reviews of others generally under various heads, an editorial article, readers' letters discussing reviews in earlier issues or scholarly points, and quick notices of lesser books. There are also publishers' advertisements, notices of job vacancies in libraries, and auction sales, etc. The *TLS* is a must, although books are reviewed too tardily for advance ordering.

Figure 9   A locating tool for book-guides, the British Council's
Aids in the selection of books

number of which are listed in the 'Guide to further reading', on p 148) include considerable treatment of book-guides. More general books on librarianship may also contain helpful sections, such as chapter 7 'Sources for the selection of books and other material' by Brian Baumfield in Lock's *Manual of library economy*. Lastly, textbooks on certain branches of librarianship, for instance children's work, together with those on subject librarianship, are further sources of information on more specialized book-guides.

Sources other than book-guides

Although book-guides are the most valuable source of information on best books, there are several other types of sources that the evaluator may turn to. This section briefly indicates what they are.

Literature guides Literature guides, already mentioned in the last section, are worthy of mention again here. Although their emphasis is on types of publications rather than on titles, they frequently name the best books on their subjects. Indeed, the titles covered by them are often given annotated entries, which means further help for the evaluator.

Subject bibliographies Book-guides, literature guides and subject bibliographies are all bibliographical publications, and it is sometimes difficult to decide which of these three types a particular published work belongs to. Subject bibliographies are essentially the type that offers least guidance on individual titles, as their main task is to aid scholars and others by listing a large number of titles. However, even subject bibliographies that are comprehensive within their scope occasionally have brief evaluative annotations, as does the science fiction bibliography by I F Clarke, *Tales of the future*, whilst some other subject bibliographies, being somewhat selective in their coverage, have longer evaluative annotations. The series of volumes that make up the *Bibliography of British history*, published at the Oxford University's Clarendon Press, are examples of such works.

State-of-the-art publications State-of-the-art publications, like the Library Association's *British librarianship and information science*, are usually published at regular intervals, and aim to give the research workers, academics, advanced students, and practitioners in the subject field, an overview of the latest discoveries and developments in the field. As discoveries and developments are reported by using the printed word, this means that state-of-the-art publications cannot help but deal, even

128

if only incidentally, with the subject's literature, and especially the recent important writings on the subject. A state-of-the-art publication that the evaluator may particularly find of value, as its subject is itself literature, is the *Year's work in English studies*.[14]

Standard works   Standard works (which were defined in chapter 2) are usually strong on bibliographical information, and this may include some selection and comments on the subject's most significant books. For example, the *Oxford history of England* series' authors do this, and A J P Taylor, in his *England, 1914-1945*, might be cited as a series' author who does it particularly well. Standard works also make up most of the titles within the next two more specialized headings.

Literary histories and form studies   The best books of the past are the ones most likely to be included in and commented upon by histories of the literature of different countries, such as Sampson's *Concise Cambridge history of English literature*, and in the histories of different forms of literature. These literary histories are of most use to the evaluator of imaginative literature. As well as histories of literary forms there are also critical studies relating to them like Margery Fisher's *Intent upon reading: a critical appraisal of modern fiction for children*. These may prove even more valuable to the evaluator.

Author studies   The literary reference books about authors mentioned in chapter 4 are not the only kind of work dealing with authors that the evaluator may turn to for critical comments. There are studies which are basically biographical, such as Frank MacShane's *The life of Raymond Chandler*, but which include comments on the author's writings. There are ones which are basically literary criticism, and deal with an authors's writings (rather than with the author himself). These the evaluator may find too detailed and specialized in their approach for his purposes, on the other hand they may have features of especial value as, for example, the references to book reviews in Sagar's study of the work of the poet Ted Hughes, *The art of Ted Hughes*. There are, of course, author studies that deal both with the author and with his works. A series of pamphlets that do this, and in which there is also detailed bibliographical information accompanying each study, is the *Writers and their work* series published by Longman for the British Council.

Notes and references

1 This information comes mainly in the form of publishers' catalogues and other handouts about current or forthcoming publi-

cations. Publishers' stocklists, which give information about all the titles available from a publisher, are usually less descriptive and may be mere cheklists.

2 Like much publishers' publicity material, these advertisement pages are also a good source of information about forthcoming publications. The *Bookseller* complements the advertisements by individual publishers in its Spring and Autumn Export numbers by having text-pages with a subject descriptive approach.

3 Although this format is not very commonly used, it has certain advantages for the librarian. For example, in an academic library where stock selection is the joint responsibility of the library and the academic staff, the individual slips can be easily passed on by the librarian to the appropriate academic staff members for their comments.

4 Of course, survey-reviews are not concerned with recent books normally, but with best books. Sources of survey-reviews are therefore dealt with in this chapter on page 118.

5 He may also learn about them by reading relevant textbooks like those on book selection cited in the 'Guide to further reading' on page 148, and by reading articles like 'Reviewing reviews' in the May 1981 issue of *Signal*.

6 *Ulrich's international periodicals directory* New York, Bowker, 1932- . Published every two or three years and supplemented in between editions by *Ulrich's quarterly* since 1977.

7 Gray, R C *A guide to book review citations: a bibliography of sources* Ohio State University Press, 1968.

8 The citation form of index, such as the *Arts and humanities citation index*, draws together all the references by other authors to a particular author's work.

9 The January 1980 issue of the *British book news* includes a list of its survey-reviews for the years 1975-9.

10 British Council and National Book League *Aids in the selection of British books* London, British Council, 1974.

11 National Book League, School Library Association, and Library Association (Youth Libraries Group) *Guides to book selection* London, NBL, SLA and LA(YLG), 1979.

12 Association for Library Service to Children, and Young Adult Services Division, American Library Association *Selecting materials for children and young adults: a bibliography of bibliographies and review sources* Chicago, American Library Association, 1980 (revised).

13 *Bibliographic index* New York, H W Wilson Co, 1938- (3 a year).

14 *Year's work in English studies* London, John Murray for the English Association, 1921- (annual).

Chapter 7

EVALUATION IN THE BOOK WEEDING PROCESS

Assessment and reassessment

Although the methods and criteria put forward in these pages can only be applied to a limited extent to the book weeding process (as carried out by libraries), the subject is, nevertheless, covered briefly here because the weeding process results in another fundamental evaluation. This time the book is evaluated in relation to its being kept (as opposed to its being bought). It is an assessment complementary, in fact, to the one carried out at the book selection stage. Basically, it is a re-assessment, and as such calls for both the criteria of assessment chosen, and the examination methods adopted, to be appropriately modified.

The weeding of books may be defined as the act of deciding which items at present in the main stock of the library should be kept where they are, and which should be removed. Those items removed will not necessarily be thrown away, but may be transfered, for example to a reserve stock. Obviously, therefore, book weeding is related to such library practices as stock control, stock maintenance, stock revision and stock withdrawal. A few libraries, notably national ones, will hardly be concerned with book weeding, as one of their main objectives is the long-term preservation of a nation's literature, but most libraries need to pay almost as much attention to book weeding as they do to book selection.

For further information on the weeding of books, most textbooks on book selection will be found worth consulting. Also worth consulting is the American monograph *Weeding library collections* by S J Slote.[1] This work concentrates on analysing the subject of weeding, not from the individual title viewpoint adopted here, but from a total library collection viewpoint, and it reveals how statistics and mathematics can aid book weeding.[2]

The criteria relevant to book weeding can be divided into two broad categories, those relevant to book evaluation generally (and therefore

132

already dealt with in this book), and those additional criteria that are relevant just to book weeding. The first category, because it is also used at the book selection stage in the life of the book, may be entitled 'Original criteria'.

Original criteria

These need not be dealt with individually again, having been dealt with in chapters 4 and 5. However, each of the seven group headings used for criteria will be surveyed and any new factors affecting them considered.

People (see also pp66-71) The most important new factor within this group of criteria relates to the author. Since the book was added to the library's stock, the standing of the author may have changed considerably, probably as a result of what he has since had published, and this change in standing may obviously affect the decision as to whether to weed.

Plan (see also pp72-4) There are no new factors to be commented on under this heading, except that the publisher may have issued one or more related works since the title under consideration was bought. Nevertheless, the criteria within it are important at the weeding stage just as they were important at the selection stage. For example, it is the book's plan which suggests if it is a work of an ephemeral nature, or one which, like a standard work, has more permanent appeal and so should be kept.

Contents (see also pp83-103) It is the criterion of up-to-dateness that is obviously particularly relevant at the time of weeding. How out of date the book has now become can be approached from three angles, at least in the case of information books. First, as regards factual content, the evaluator must ask the question: is the factual content of the work now so dated as to be positively misleading? Second, the ideas and thought patterns of the book must be considered and the question asked: are they still acceptable to the average library reader? Third, the author's vocabulary and style must be studied and the question put: are they such that they can still appeal to readers?

Organization (see also pp75-6) There are no new factors under this group heading, and the criteria within it are not likely to affect any decision about the weeding of the book. However, new editions of books, especially quick-reference books, are occasionally organized quite differently from their previous editions, and sometimes much less efficiently. When this happens, old editions have to be kept.

Design (pp76-8) The criteria under this heading, like those under the last, will deldom affect any decision made about a book at the weeding stage.

Production (see also pp78-9) The quality of the original materials and workmanship must obviously affect the condition of a used book, but generally the criteria related to the production of a book are not otherwise important when it is being considered for weeding.

Placing (pp79-80) The placing of a publication is clearly changed by the publication of comparable works. It is also affected by the production of later editions of the work itself. Most libraries weed out old editions of a book when a new one is bought, but since old editions sometimes contain whole subject areas that have been omitted for some reason from the later editions, they can then be of much more than just historical value.

It should be noted also that the usefulness of a book may change rather than diminish over the years. For example, directories very soon go out of date and are then useless for the purpose for which they were published. Yet old directories are invaluable in historical research.

Finally, it should be remembered that the placing of a library book that has reached its weeding stage is further affected by what similar works, if any, the library has in stock. The library evaluator, in book weeding as in book selection, must always place the book in the context of his own collection.

Additional criteria

There are four very important criteria that must be taken into account that are unique to the book weeding process, and must be given individual treatment.

Use This is an obvious criterion, but it should be borne in mind that the work will not only have been used by the library's readers, but possibly lent to other libraries to be read by their borrowers. It may also have been used, for one reason or another, by the library staff. It is the total use of the work that the evaluator needs to measure as accurately as he can. However, a book needs not only to have been used but to be still in use for it to be kept on the library's main shelves. Furthermore, the evaluator should estimate, if he can, its future use. It can be assumed that the average book will be used less and less as it increases in age.

The most valuable information about use is obviously contained on the date labels of books. However, not all books have them (those in

134

reference departments commonly lack them), whilst some books have been used so much that they have had more than one lable. Of the dates on date labels, the most significant are the last few, for it is the time interval between the publication's last three or four issue dates, together with the date of its last issue, that indicates how weedable it is. Of course, in the case of specialized works or works rated as being of lasting worth, the use can reasonably be found to be less than that of popular titles, but any publication that has not been used for two years can probably be weeded.

Condition The physical condition of a book is certainly going to deteriorate the more it is used, and many books are weeded because they have become worn out. The librarian's problem is when he cannot replace a title still in demand because it is out of print. (Often, however, books in poor condition are also poorly used, because their physical condition puts readers off them.) If the evaluator wishes to retain a book that is in poor condition because it is impossible to replace it, he may decide to have it repaired, microcopied, or even photocopied. He may also have photocopies made just of missing or damaged pages, so that the work can be kept.

Availability This criterion is made up of several factors, and may be analysed by dividing it into market availability and library availability. Market availability is whether copies of the title are still on sale in any form. Sometimes otherwise out of print works are available in microform. However, even when a book is not available for purchase in any form from a publisher, it may still be obtained second hand. Library availability is made up of internal factors and external ones. The internal ones are whether the library has other copies of the title in stock, perhaps somewhere else within its system, and whether these other copies can be made easily available. The external ones relate to whether, if the library no longer has a copy of the title in its own stock and cannot replace it, it can be borrowed, preferably quickly, from another library. Obviously old, rare, and valuable out of print works are the least likely to be available from external sources.

Published guidelines Several types of guidelines may be made use of (though some only occasionally), such as the published evaluations covered in chapter 6. Of these, the category concerned with best books will be found the most relevant to book weeding, since it is good books that libraries most need to keep in stock. Especially relevant are those lists of titles that particular kinds of libraries should stock. It may, in fact, be a library's policy to keep on its shelves all the titles on certain such lists.

Related to this kind of list are guidelines and standards put out by professional bodies. Often these guidelines will just suggest the sort of titles which should be stocked rather than give a full list of titles, as does the recent Library Association *Guidelines for reference and information services to public libraries in England and Wales.*[3] However, even this limited kind of guidance is of real help.

A second form of guideline which may be used is that which relates to a single library system, though admittedly it may be hard to obtain as it may not be published in a formal way. This type of guideline can be of several different kinds, the most obvious being the list issued by the central book services section of the library, laying down what titles each service point must stock. These lists will normally be limited to a particular kind of book. To take the example of reference books again, the Lancashire Library issues a list of reference works that must be stocked by its branches.[4]

A sort of guideline as to what books to keep in a particular academic library are an institution's own reading lists put out by its staff for student use. Clearly the library must retain on its shelves copies of all works being currently recommended for use in the institution's courses.

A third type of guideline takes the form of citation analyses, including citation indexes such as the *Social science citation index.*[5] Such analyses indicate how much individual publications are still being cited by writers, and therefore suggest in a general way whether a particular publication is likely to be used if retained on a library's shelves.

Examination

The examination of a book at the weeding stage is normally a brief one, similar to the Experienced Glance. However, because its purpose is to decide whether to keep a book as opposed to whether to buy one, it has a character of its own. There are four stages to the weeding examination.

Familiarization This is the act of finding out something about the book, so that the decision to weed (or not) is based on reasonable knowledge. If the book is one already known to the evaluator, and its being in his library's stock may well mean it is, then noting the author and title details on the spine of the book may be all that is needed in the way of familiarization. But if the book is not known to the evaluator he will have at least to examine its title leaf, its contents page, and quickly glance at its textmatter. This will enable him to sum

136

up the type of book he is dealing with, as well as revealing its overall contents and features.

Use   The second stage is to establish how much the work has been used.   As most library books contain date labels, a record of use is easily ascertained. With books that have had more than one date label, a record of the number of issues stamped on the previous one(s) may be recorded by the library on the rear of the title page leaf. If a book's use is not recorded in any way, its condition will give some indication of its use. In addition, the evaluator may be able to estimate its approximate use because of his own past handling of the work. It should be noted that in those libraries where reference books are given date labels, the record of use on them (at least with open-shelf works) will be incomplete, as readers often return these books to the shelves even though they are asked to leave them on the tables to be stamped.

Condition   The condition of the book will have probably been noticed in a general way by the evaluator while he is carrying out the first two stages of the weeding examination. However, the physical condition of the book needs to be investigated systematically. The evaluator should first look at the state of the book's cover, to see how worn and dirty it is. He should then examine the end-paper hinges, which will possibly be coming apart, and also look at the sewing of the sections, which may be working loose. He should finally flick through the pages, looking at the condition of the paper, and noting any dirty marks and damage. Whilst doing this, he should ascertain that no pages or illustrations are missing.

Comparisons   The last stage in the examination is comparing the book with other copies of the work on the library shelves, and with books on similar subjects. If there are further copies of the same title available, the question to be asked by the evaluator is: are these copies identical to the one under examination, or are they different versions or editions of the title? If they are later editions, then the edition under examination can normally be weeded, but a careful check is needed first to see that the later edition retains all the features of the earlier one. If the other copies are identical, their comparative condition must be judged, so that if any weeding is needed, the worst copy is the one that is weeded. The use made of the other copies should be ascertained at the same time, for it is the total use of all the library's copies of a publication which indicates how many are needed.

If there are no other copies of the same work in stock, the question to be asked is: are there publications, especially more recent ones, that cover virtually the same subject in virtually the same way? If there are, the book under examination can probably be weeded.

Post-examination decisions

If, after the examination, the evaluator is not sure whether or not to weed a book, he should ask the advice of other members of the library staff before he comes to his decision. In a library situation, the evaluator can choose to do a wide range of things with a book that he has decided to weed. Obviously, he can discard it, possibly deciding at the same time to buy a replacement copy. If he decides to discard, he may then assess that its condition is good enough for it to be put on sale to readers (this is becoming a common public library practice), rather than just go for pulping.

But many books that are weeded are not discarded, merely transferred or repaired. A book may be transferred from the main stock to a reserve stock; it may be transferred to another service point; it may be transferred to another type of use (ie from reference to lending); or it may be transferred to another library system altogether.

A book may be repaired in two main ways. If only minor repair is necessary the library staff will undertake this, but books which need more major repair work, such as rebinding, are sent to library binders.

Obviously the evaluator's decisions as to what to do with books that he has decided to weed will be affected by such factors as the policies and practices of the library in which he is working. These factors may be outside his control, but they must influence his judgement.

Notes and references

1 Slote, S J *Weeding library collections* Littleton, Libraries Unlimited, 1975 (Research studies in library science, no. 14).

2 The name now often given to such mathematical and statistical studies when they concern literature and libraries is bibliometrics.

3 Library Association *Guidelines for reference and information services to public libraries in England and Wales* London, Library Association, 1981. Appendix 1: Guidelines to provision of reference materials.

4 Lancashire Library *Standards for reference and information services* 1978. Appendix 2: Reference works.

5 Institute for Scientific Information *Social science citation index* Philadelphia, ISI, 1973- (3 a year).

Chapter 8

BOOKS COMPARED WITH OTHER MATERIALS

This chapter briefly considers how book evaluation methods compare with those called for when other library materials are being dealt with, and shows how the systematic method of evaluation can be extended and applied not only to the other printed materials that libraries stock but also to non-print materials. Those stages of the systematic method that deal with establishing criteria and examination procedures can be modified to meet the evaluation needs of published materials other than books.

The materials that libraries stock, in addition to books, are extremely wide ranging. Some, like manuscripts and other unpublished and archive materials, are outside normal selection and evaluation procedures because of their nature, and so will be excluded here. However, all published library materials can be systematically evaluated by the method described in chapter 3. Every one of the twelve stages delineated there is relevant to other library materials and so the evaluator's framework when assessing them will be as for books: Objectives; Strategy; Background reading; Criteria; Examination; Matching; Comparable publications; Personal conclusions; Obtaining second opinions; Obtaining further information; Final results; Applying results.

Obviously, however, the detailed decisions and procedures called for within the framework will vary, depending on what type of library material the evaluator is dealing with. Basically, there are four groups of published library materials, and which group the material falls in determines more than anything else the detailed decisions and procedures necessary.

The first group consists of printed non-book materials, including such publications as periodicals and newspapers and, as might be expected, necessitates the least modification in evaluation methods. The second group is that of non-print or audio-visual materials, which are materials viewed or heard (or both) rather than read, such as gramo-

139

phone records, video-recordings and films. Needless to say the methods of evaluation used will need to be adapted to accommodate their special features. The third group of library materials consists of those that are by nature a cross between the first two. Microforms come into this category because while physically they are filmlike, they are designed in the main to be read. Posters, maps and similar visual materials can also be considered part of this group as, though they are essentially designed to be looked at, they are printed, usually on paper, and may have in part to be read. The last group comprises those publications, sometimes called multi-media publications, that have both printed and audio-visual components. For example, those published language courses that consist of a mixture of textbooks and sound recordings belong to this group.

Although it is hoped that the evaluator will find the comparisons and comments made in this chapter helpful in his evaluation of non-book materials, it is recommended that he refer for more detailed guidance to textbooks on these materials. He may also find useful those titles listed under the heading 'Book selection' in the further reading section on p148, as most cover a wide range of library materials.

Criteria

All the seven group headings used for criteria discussed earlier can be used with any kind of published material. The individual criteria within the seven headings, however, will need some expanding, even when evaluating printed non-book materials such as periodicals, whilst two additional group headings are called for to cater satisfactorily for the assessment of all other materials.

People (see also pp66-71) As with books, there are authors, editors, artists, designers and publishers (or producing organizations) connected with most other types of library materials, including audio-visual ones. Also involved, however, are appropriate technical experts, as well as the firms which actually make the materials, (which usually come from several industries and not just the printing industry). In the case of the periodicals there are the referees[1] to be considered, whilst with most audio-visual materials performers such as musicians and actors are involved.

Plan (see also pp72-4) Just as individual books may t related to other books, and possibly issued in alternative versions, so may individual titles belonging to all other categories of library materials. For instance, a film might be made available both in 16mm and 35mm.

140

In fact, the criteria relating to the plan of a book are overall very applicable to other library materials, although sometimes further criteria need considering as, for example, that of frequency in the case of newspapers and periodicals.

Contents (see also pp83-103) Looking first at printed non-book materials, periodicals and newspapers are probably the most important types of these in libraries. Although the contents of some titles within this type contain (in whole or in part) fictional items, their contents in the main are, like information books, factual. This means that the criteria applicable to information books are the ones most relevant to them. There are, however, many different kinds of periodicals and the evaluator must be prepared to adapt his criteria as appropriate. He should also be aware that evaluating newspapers and periodicals calls for several additional criteria under this heading: for example, advertisements are an important feature of most newspapers and periodicals, as are abstracts[2] in scholarly journals.

Turning to the contents of audio-visual materials, if these are works of the imagination such as feature films, the criteria laid down for fiction books are, of course, the ones on which to base any assessment. However, many audio-visual materials are informational and educational in nature, and so should be treated as are the contents of information books. The precise criteria that are relevant to audio-visual materials obviously depend to a large extent on whether they are audio or visual or both. Whilst with audio materials it is necessary to have additional criteria for such features as sound effects, it is necessary with visual ones to have them for features like captions and stills.

Interpretation and performance The interpretation and performance of the script and/or score of such audio-visual materials as, for instance, films and sound recordings, are also subject to evaluation, and form a group heading of their own. (The term 'production' is not used here, having earlier been used in respect of physical form and make-up.)

Several criteria come within this group heading, such as acting, camerawork, lighting, and special effects, though the actual criteria that need to be considered will depend on the type of audio-visual material under evaluation. Most of the criteria that relate to interpretation and performance have both artistic and technical aspects to them. For example, an opera singer recording an aria will need, in order to do it successfully, not only to have a voice which is trained in the techniques of singing, but also to have the artistic ability to convey the full meaning of the aria.

Organization (pp75-6) The arrangement and indexing of printed non-book material is important as it is with books. When looking at newspapers and periodicals, the evaluator should consider dividing the indexing criterion into two, and have one for internal indexes (ie the periodical's own, if any) and another for external indexes (ie the indexing services such as the *British humanities index*, which index, in whole or in part, the contents of periodicals).

Although many periodicals have both their own indexes and are in addition indexed by indexing services, few audio-visual materials are indexed in any way, for their nature does not lend itself to indexing. However, there is no reason why they should not be at least as well arranged and guided as possible. How this is best done depends on what kind of material they are. Overall, audio-visual material is undoubtedly much harder to refer to quickly than printed material.

Design (see also pp76-8) The design criteria in printed non-book materials are essentially the same as those in books themselves, simply because the design problems faced are the same — the placing of print on paper in a manner both effective and pleasing. However, the design problems with audio-visual materials are rather different and the design factors (at least with visual materials) need to be divided into two. First, there are those that are concerned with the design of the actual interpretation and performance of the contents matter, such as the film-set of a film. Second are those more like the design factors in printed materials, that is the ones that are concerned with the design of the physical medium carrying the contents and its packaging, for example, how a set of photographic slides are mounted, boxed and labelled.

Production (see also pp78-9) The methods employed to make the publication a physical object, together with the materials used, and the craftsmanship found, must be first evaluated, for example, the quality of the pressing of a gramophone record. Next, those to do with the boxing and labelling of the publication should be examined, for instance, whether the record sleeve successfully protects the gramophone record itself.

The methods, materials and craftsmanship part of this group of criteria is particularly important with microforms, as poor photography and reproduction cause librarians and their readers additional legibility problems to those already inherent in the medium.

Placing (see also pp79-80) All the criteria relevant to the placing of a book are applicable with the addition that a comparison of the various interpretations and performances of a work that are available for purchase should be made. (The reviewers of audio-visual materials[3] frequently concentrate on such comparisons.)

Equipment This additional heading is obviously not applicable to any printed materials as no special equipment is needed to use them. However, it is relevant to the other three goups of library materials which depend upon such equipment as tape recorders and film projectors for their utilization. The equipment needs to be evaluated before being purchased by a library, and while common items such as record players and slide projectors will play or project most of the materials that are published, libraries sometimes find the the item they are interested in is not compatible with the equipment they possess. For example, a film may be only available on 35mm and the library may only possess 8mm and 16mm projectors. The equipment needed to show such things as films is often referred to as hardware, whilst the materials themselves (ie the films) are referred to as software.

Examination

The need for equipment like projectors to be on hand before audio-visual materials can be examined, coupled with the nature of the materials, means that it is generally practicable to do nothing less than a full examination of them (see pp46-8). However, of the other two kinds of examination mentioned in chapter 3, the longer, the Skilful Skim, may sometimes be carried out. The shorter, the Experienced Glance, is not possible with audio-visual materials, although a substitute for it is occasionally possible. This takes the form of studying the information given about the particular title on the printed matter which accompanies it. The outstanding example of a type of audio-visual material with informative printed matter accompanying it is the gramophone record, whose sleeve often has its back filled with relevant facts. Skilful skims can be carried out with some audio-visual materials, such as filmstrips, by viewing them in a limited way with the naked eye, allowing a fairly quick if rather rough assessment.

A full examination of an audio-visual item cannot be divided into the three stages relevant to examining a book (preview, view and review) because of the limitations of the equipment it utilizes. Browsing is seldom possible and only the middle and main stages are really practicable, though of course the whole item can be played again as necessary. However, all the four steps that make up this stage of the full examination process can be carried out: deciding on the arrangement of any notes that are to be made; noting down the bibliographical details of the item (obviously these will vary depending on what type of audio-visual material is under examination); hearing and/or seeing it; and, finally, carrying out appropriate tests and analyses. This last step may prove difficult for the same reason as previewing and reviewing of audio-visual materials is difficult. They cannot be referred to and browsed through as easily as printed materials.

With multi-media packs each part must be fully examined, together with any printed notes supplied with the pack. With some, for instance tape-slide units, the printed notes may be quite detailed, possibly giving the full script of the words spoken in it.

Thus, the examination of audio-visual materials is not only different from that of books, it is also more difficult. On the other hand, the examination of printed non-book materials like periodicals is comparatively straightforward and can, indeed, be carried out very much as a book examination. Of course, because the actual component parts of printed non-book publications differ from those of books (for example, newspapers do not have dust jackets), the evaluator must adapt his examination of a particular item to the type of material it is. In addition, with newspapers and periodicals, he should not normally judge the title on the examination of a single issue, but try to see at least half a dozen issues of the title. For example, with a daily newspaper, he should examine those covering a whole week.

Notes and references

1 Referees are the subject experts who, with periodicals of a learned or research nature, are sent copies of articles being considered for publication. Their task is to assess the subject content of the articles and indicate whether or not they consider them worthy of publication.

2 Abstracts are summaries of articles and other writings. They are not normally evaluative. They will be found not only accompanying the writings themselves, but in such abstracting services as *Chemical abstracts.*

3 Examples of such reviews for gramophone records will be found in Lade, J, ed. *Building a library 2* (Oxford University Press, 1980). These reviews are ones originally broadcast on the BBC's Radio 3.

Appendix

CHECKLISTS OF CRITERIA FOR INFORMATION BOOKS
AND FOR FICTION

Checklist for information books
The references are to where the criteria are discussed in chapters 4 and 5.

1 *People* (see pp66-71)
(a) Author
(b) Editor etc.
(c) Artists and photographers
(d) Designer
(e) Printer etc.
(f) Publisher

2 *Plan* (see pp72-4)
(a) Subject or theme
(b) Origins
(c) Aim
(d) Audience
(e) Variant issues
(f) Special services
(g) Related works

3 *Contents* (see pp84-93)
(a) Standing
(b) Research: methods and sources
(c) Soundness
(d) Length
(e) Scope
(f) Detail
(g) Viewpoint
(h) Bias
(i) Balance
(j) Level
(k) Style
(l) Accuracy
(m) Up-to-dateness
(n) Revision
(o) Permanence
(p) Bibliographical information
(q) Visual information
(r) Special features
(s) Supporting material
(t) Effect

4 *Organization* (see pp75-6)
(a) Arrangement
(b) Contents list
(c) Indexes
(d) Cross-references
(e) Headings

5 *Design* (see pp76-8)
(a) Format
(b) Layout
(c) Legibility
(d) Aesthetic aspects

6 *Production* (see pp78-9)
(a) Methods
(b) Craftsmanship
(c) Materials

7 *Placing* (see pp79-80)
(a) Price
(b) Comparisons
(c) Uniqueness
(d) Quality
(e) Usefulness

Checklist for fiction
The references are to where the criteria are discussed in chapters 4 and 5.

1 *People* (see pp66-71)
(a) Author
(b) Editor etc.
(c) Artists and photographers
(d) Designer
(e) Printer etc.
(f) Publisher

2 *Plan* (see pp72-4)
(a) Subject or theme
(b) Origins
(c) Aim
(d) Audience
(e) Variant issues
(f) Special services
(g) Related works

3 *Contents* (see pp93-102)
(a) Standing
(b) Research: methods and sources
(c) Observation
(d) Inventiveness
(e) Length
(f) Plot
(g) Setting
(h) Characters
(i) Level
(j) Approach

(k) Style
(l) Spirit
(m) Permanence
(n) Visual information

(o) Supporting material
(p) Effect
(q) Power

4 *Organization* (see pp75-6)
(a) Arrangement
(b) Contents list
(c) Indexes

(d) Cross-references
(e) Headings

5 *Design* (see pp76-8)
(a) Format
(b) Layout

(c) Legibility
(d) Aesthetic aspects

6 *Production* (see pp78-9)
(a) Methods
(b) Craftsmanship

(c) Materials

7 *Placing* (see pp79-80)
(a) Price
(b) Comparisons
(e) Uniqueness

(d) Quality
(e) Usefulness

GUIDE TO FURTHER READING

In addition to the suggestions for reading, mainly relating to specific topics, already given in the *Notes and references*, there are a number of books on more general subjects which are also recommended.

Book-making

Jennett, S *The making of books* 5th ed. London, Faber and Faber, 1973. This standard work was written for authors, and covers both book design and book production.

McMurtrie, D C *The book: the story of printing and bookmaking* New York, Oxford University Press, 1943. Last reprinted in 1977, this is a classic work which gives most emphasis to the historical aspects of book-making.

The book world

Baker, J *The book business* London, John Baker, 1971. A short work but with coverage of most aspects of its subject.

Blond, A *The publishing game* London, Cape, 1971. An easy to read introduction to the book world.

Colby, J P *Writing, illustrating and editing children's books* New York, Hastings House, 1967. Gives considerable insight into more specialized aspects of the book world.

Book selection

In addition to the titles below, two classics of the subject may also still be found of value. They are F K W Drury's *Book selection* (Chicago, American Library Association, 1930) and *Living with books* by Helen Haines (New York, Columbia University Press, 1950).

Bonk, W J and Magrill, R M *Building library collections* 5th ed. Metuchen, Scarecrow Press, 1979. A revision of the work originally by Carter and Bonk, and a wide-ranging title.

Broadus, R N *Selecting material for libraries* 2nd ed. New York, H W Wilson, 1981. A detailed treatment of the subject with considerable information on individual subject fields.

Cabeceiras, J *The multimedia library: materials selection and use* New York, Academic Press, 1978. Evaluation emphasized more than in most works on book selection. Covers not only books, but a wide variety of library materials.

Katz, W A *Collection development: the selection of materials for libraries* New York, Holt, Rinehart and Winston, 1980. The author has written other good books, this one deals well with the selection of most library materials.

Spiller, D *Book selection* 3rd ed. London, Bingley, 1980. The only current British work on the subject; this edition is the best so far.

Van Orden, P and Phillips, E B, eds. *Background readings in building library collections* 2nd ed. Metuchen, Scarecrow Press, 1979. A collection of articles, some on evaluation.

Book reviewing

Kamerman, S E, ed. *Book reviewing: a guide to writing book reviews for newspapers, magazines, radio and television* Boston, The Writer, 1978. The contributions to this work vary in quality, but some are good, and evaluation is reasonably covered.

Merritt, L C, Boaz, M, and Tisdel, K S *Reviews in library book selection* Detroit, Wayne State University Press, 1958. In spite of now being rather dated, it is still of value as its treatment of reviewing is related to library needs.

Oppenheimer, E *Oral book reviewing to stimulate reading: a practical guide in technique for lecture and broadcast* Metuchen, Scarecrow Press, 1980. Treatment of a specialized area of reviewing which all book evaluators should be aware of.

Critical reading

Adler, M J and Van Doren, C *How to read a book* Revised ed. New York, Simon and Schuster, 1972. A comprehensive guide to intelligent and critical reading.

Flower, F *Reading to learn: an approach to critical reading* London, BBC publications, 1969. Introduces both critical reading and the study of literature.

149

Literary criticism

Bateson, F W *The scholar-critic: an introduction to literary research* London, Routledge and Kegan Paul, 1972. Deals both with literary scholarship and with literary criticism.

Roberts, M *The fundamentals of literary criticism* Oxford, Blackwell, 1974. Aimed at the beginner, deals systematically with the critical process.

Smith, L H *The unreluctant years: a critical approach to children's literature* Chicago, American Library Association, 1953. This publication is probably the one that comes nearest to examining literary criticism in relation to children's books.

INDEX

Excluded are the illustrations and those authors and titles that are merely named, not commented upon.